MW01517409

Supervisory Techniques for the Security Professional

Supervisory Techniques for the Security Professional

JOHN A. WANAT
Vice President
Centurion Training Institute
Montclair, New Jersey

EDWARD T. GUY
Director of Support Services
Rahway Hospital
Rahway, New Jersey

JOHN J. MERRIGAN, JR.
Loss Prevention Specialist
   and Consultant
Bradenton Beach, Florida

Butterworth–Heinemann

Boston   London   Oxford   Singapore   Sydney   Toronto   Wellington

Library of Congress Cataloging in Publication Data

Wanat, John A.
    Supervisory techniques for the security
professional.

    Bibliography: p.
    Includes index.
    1. Police, Private—Personnel management.
2. Security consultants.   3. Supervision of police
personnel.   4. Industry—Security measures. I. Guy,
Edward T., 1938–   .   II. Merrigan, John J.,
1937–   .   III. Title.
HV8081.W28   363.2'89'0683   81–1180
ISBN 0-7506-9271-5 (previously ISBN 0-409-95035-1)   AACR2

Butterworth–Heinemann
80 Montvale Avenue
Stoneham, MA 02180

Printed in the United States of America

To Security Professionals Everywhere

Contents

Foreword

During the past decade we have seen Security come of age. Progress in the field can be noted in several ways—one of the most notable is the amount of material available in our field of interest to assist the practitioner in developing and implementing sound protection systems. We have developed voluminous material to assist in training the Security Officer. With extensive training efforts directed to the officer we, as a field of expertise, have neglected the training and upgrading of one of the most important elements of any system—the competent Supervisor.

The Supervisor is the person who actually makes the program "go", yet our failure rate in terms of the supervisor who did not make it is rather dismal. All too often, an individual who has been an outstanding Security Officer is promoted into Supervision and destined for failure. The reason being is that he seldom has been given the necessary training beforehand and rarely has been given the crucial continuing developmental training to enhance his effectiveness.

It is true that we have not had material which has directly addressed the specifics we were seeking. This text, *SUPERVISORY TECHNIQUES FOR THE SECURITY PROFESSIONAL,* now fills a void providing an opportunity for Security to further come of age as we move into the eighties. The effective supervisor is a key element in the successful security protection program.

Russell Colling
Director of Security and Safety
Hospital Shared Services of Colorado

Preface

Modern security professionals have important supervisory functions to perform in today's complex security field. In order to keep pace with this expanding field, the security professional must be experienced in the technical aspects of the security profession as well as with the current techniques of effective supervision.

This book, then, is written to assist the recently appointed security professional in succeeding in his supervisory role, while also providing the experienced security professional with helpful principles and techniques to become a more effective supervisor. It is a practical, workable and up-to-date guide for security professionals interested in improving themselves and the field they serve.

Unique features of this book include:

- Supervisory Development chapters dealing with Management Techniques; Leadership Development; Effective Communications; Delegating Authority and Control; Handling Complaints and Grievances; and Ethics.
- A chapter on Training Skill Development that contains helpful hints on involving security professionals in the total training function.
- Time-saving techniques to assist security professionals in maximizing their efficiency and output.
- Self-evaluating checklists at the conclusion of each chapter to assist security professionals in identifying their strengths and weaknesses.
- Tips on conducting safety inspections and accident investigations.
- Step-by-step procedures in identifying and implementing a positive public relations program.

We wish to acknowledge the American Society for Industrial Security, ASIS, and the International Association for Hospital Security, IAHS, for permission to reproduce their material. We express our sincere gratitude to all those who have assisted us in preparing this text, and a special thanks to Russell Colling.

1

Leadership Development

Many people associate leadership with the position one holds in an organization. This is particularly true of the security profession since it has a military rank structure. They assume that if an individual is a sergeant, a lieutenant, a captain, or the security director, then that person must be a leader. This assumption should not be universally applied. Certainly one would hope and expect the security supervisory and managerial staff to be leaders, but their rank alone does not make them so.

The rank one holds in the organization simply indicates a position one has obtained in the hierarchical structure of the security profession. As security supervisors, these individuals may or may not have leadership ability.

What constitutes a leader? Is it the ability to give orders? A parent can order a child to do his or her bidding, but this alone does not make the parent a leader. The sheer size and strength of the adult can be overpowering to the youngster, who will submit to the adult's orders.

Is it communication? A telephone operator earns a weekly paycheck by communicating. However, the operator may not have any leadership ability.

Is it authority? Authority is frequently associated with a leader. But authority does not make a leader. The boss's son may inherit the business, and have the authority to direct the company operations, but he may not have the managerial skills or the leadership ability to be successful in this.

The above examples are oversimplifications of our point. No *one* characteristic or trait makes an effective leader. It is usually a combination of acceptable qualities, characteristics and traits that distinguish a leader from a non-leader.

Not all leadership qualities are inborn. Many can be developed through instruction, self-awareness and practice. This chapter will deal with the qualities, characteristics and traits of an effective leader. First we will define leadership, and then we will identify the various types of leadership styles. After discussing the positive and negative aspects of leadership styles, we will focus on the self-awareness and goal-setting functions that will assist the security supervisor in overcoming any leadership shortcomings.

Leadership is defined by the Air Force as the "act of influencing and directing people in a way that will win their obedience, confidence, respect, and loyal cooperation in achieving a common objective.'' (Leadership in the Air Force (2 B-2).[1]

In essence, leadership is the ability and readiness to inspire, direct, and influence the actions of others. To lead means to guide or show the way. A leader is a person who influences or guides the decisions or actions of others. Every security supervisor must have leadership ability in order to carry out his assignments and functions.

TYPES OF LEADERSHIP

Two types of leadership are usually found in the organizational structure—formal leadership and informal leadership.

Formal leadership is the position occupied by and actions taken by persons designated to perform certain leadership functions in a formal organizational structure. It is the position and function of elected or appointed officers. The duties, responsibilities, and authority of formal leadership in organizations are usually stated in writing and are clear.

Informal leadership, on the other hand, is the position of leader bestowed upon a person by his peers because of the respect they have for that person's ability and readiness to lead. This kind of leadership functions in all groups that have freedom of action. It is the driving force of nearly all group action. It comes from the composition of the group.

This chapter concerns itself with the formal type of leadership. Security supervisors are designated by management to carry out specific duties and assignments. They are also given the appropriate authority to accomplish company security objectives.

CATEGORIES OF LEADERSHIP

There are essentially three categories of leadership; authoritarian, laissez-faire, and democratic. A close look at each is warranted in order to develop a style of leadership that will assist the security officer in being the best possible type of leader.

Authoritarian.   A supervisor practicing authoritarian leadership insists that his orders be followed to the letter. There is no room for deviation under the authoritarian leader. Everything must be done as ordered. In effect, authoritarian leaders impose their will on subordinates in order to accomplish a task. This type of leadership is very inflexible. The supervisor reserves all decisions to himself while directing the subordinates' actions at each and every step. In

[1]Portions of this chapter were adapted from ''Leadership in The Air Force'' and ''Military Leadership.''

effect, he is "boss" and all tasks are personally assigned by him. Praise and criticism are also highly personalized. Unquestioning obedience by subordinates of the authoritarian leader is a must.

Laissez-faire. A supervisor practicing laissez-faire leadership allows subordinates complete freedom of choice in making decisions. Although available for advice, he does not volunteer assistance or direction. Usually, someone else in the group assumes an informal leadership role. An individual practicing this type of leadership neither praises nor criticizes. Subordinates frequently become disenchanted with this obvious lack of direction and leadership.

Democratic. A supervisor engaged in democratic leadership is one who firmly believes in using group cooperation to achieve the desired goals and tasks. This type of leader is open for suggestions from the group. He offers several alternatives to the group for consideration while listening to the group for their suggestions. Subordinates under a democratic leader are free to work with whomever they please. Work loads and task assignments are pretty much left to the group to decide. The leader endeavors to be objective in both praise and criticism. The democratic leader does not expect to be known as the "boss."

Based on the above descriptions of the three types of leaders, it is obvious a security supervisor should strike a balance between the authoritative and democratic leadership styles. There are times when the security supervisor must be authoritarian in order to get the job done. Authority in itself is not bad. Most people want to be told what to do and when to do it. Authority, however, has an element of fear associated with it, and leadership based solely on fear will fail. Effective leadership requires the security supervisor to weigh each situation and choose the leadership style that will best accomplish the desired objective within the allotted time. The laissez-faire type of leadership is totally unacceptable in the security field. There is no guarantee that any action will result nor is there any guarantee that any possible action, of any quality, will be available in time to meet the needs of the group.

LEADERSHIP PRINCIPLES

Listed below are ten principles of leadership. Adherence to these principles should increase your ability to lead.

- JOB AWARENESS is essential to meeting the organization's objectives and goals. Operational procedures require job awareness and knowledge of how one function interfaces with another. Security supervisors and subordinates should be up to date on the latest developments in their field.
- SELF-AWARENESS on the part of the security supervisor is a must. Intro-

spection, an awareness of your strong and weak points, will assist supervisors in charting realistic goals and objectives as well as identifying avenues for correcting deficiencies.

- **SELF-IMPROVEMENT** must be constantly practiced. A self-improvement program should be established that takes into consideration the supervisor's physical, mental, moral, human relations and managerial improvements.
- **SUBORDINATE AWARENESS** requires that the supervisor take a genuine interest in his or her subordinates. It requires an understanding of basic psychology. The supervisor should know the name, family status, educational level, capabilities and limitations of his or her immediate subordinates.
- **COMMUNICATION** is an essential tool of an effective leader. Appropriate and sufficient information must flow up, down, and across the chain of command. Subordinates must be kept well informed, with clear and understandable directions.
- **TRAINING** is paramount to success. Performance often depends on the type of training received. Supervisors must constantly provide technical assistance, in-house training, and encouragement for subordinates to engage in professional development.
- **RESPONSIBILITY** and leadership go hand-in-hand. Supervisors should look for ways to perform the job efficiently, instead of looking for reasons why they shouldn't do it.
- **INITIATIVE** is synonymous with leadership. Seek out ways to improve operations. Be willing to accept new challenges. Don't shy away from increased responsibilities.
- **OBJECTIVITY** is required in making sound and timely decisions. All facts should be carefully and objectively considered before making a decision.
- **FAIRNESS** must be a supervisor's trademark. Favoritism and unfair work assignments must be avoided at all costs. A security supervisor should always try to be fair and just in dealing with others.

Leadership by Example

The best example is a good example. A wise supervisor will establish professional standards for his subordinates by demonstrating a positive image.

The security supervisor's actions will strongly influence the subordinates' actions. An effective leader will endeavor to demonstrate, by example, leadership characteristics such as courage, integrity, and proper personal appearance and personal conduct.

Some ways to apply this principle are:

- Be physically and mentally fit

- Be loyal to your company, your profession, your supervisors, and your subordinates
- Be fair in your dealings with others
- Be morally courageous
- Be in control of your emotions
- Be neat in appearance
- Be aware of your weak points and strive to improve them

Be a Professional

Leadership and professionalism go hand in hand. Simply being promoted into a supervisory capacity does not automatically assure the supervisor's acceptance and respect by the rank and file. The supervisor must demonstrate competence and professionalism in his or her undertakings. Failure of the security supervisor to carry out duties in a professional manner will result in a lack of confidence by subordinates.

Some techniques to develop a professional image are:

- Keep abreast of current security developments
- Actively participate in professional security organizations
- Further your educational level, take courses, attend seminars and read, read, read
- Seek out a role model and study his/her actions
- Learn from other security professionals.
- Prepare yourself to move up the ladder while preparing subordinates to fill your shoes
- Implement the professional techniques you have learned

Develop Self-confidence

Every leader must develop self-confidence. It is a realization of one's own self-worth and his ability to carry out his supervisory functions. Self-confidence is not to be confused with pompousness or overconfidence. Overconfidence can be as dangerous as lack of confidence. A true leader weighs all facts before making decisions.

To achieve self-confidence:

- Develop an optimistic outlook
- Inventory your strengths and weaknesses and strive to improve shortcomings
- Establish realistic goals and chart a course of action to reach these goals
- Take a genuine interest in people
- Listen to what others have to say, weigh their advice, and take appropriate and decisive action

Develop Teamwork

A precision drill team can function only if each and every member coordinates his routine to be in consort with each other. It is the leader's responsibility to see to it that all members act as a team. When one member does not cooperate or "fouls up," the entire team looks bad. Likewise, the security function of any organization, large or small, is built upon effective and efficient teamwork. If teamwork is not developed, the organization's security can be compromised. Therefore, the leader must emphasize the importance of each person's contribution to the security function. The more effective the teamwork, the greater the results.

You can develop teamwork if you:

- Develop an understanding of your subordinates' strengths and weaknesses, and capitalize on their strong points
- Help each member to understand the importance of their position and how it contributes to the total security operation
- Provide in-house training to support a team effort
- Keep subordinates well informed
- Provide on-the-job instruction

No one characteristic or trait makes an effective leader. It is usually a combination of acceptable characteristics and traits that distinguish a leader from a non-leader. However, a glaring fault in an individual's leadership style will often override good points, and decrease the individual's leadership effectiveness. A wise leader will assess his strong and weak points and strengthen those that need reinforcement.

Leadership must be constant; it cannot be turned on and off. A security officer has a professional responsibility to practice effective leadership at all times. The principles of leadership are virtually meaningless unless the supervisor applies them. Through self-training and practice, each security officer must plan his personal leadership development program. Figures 1-1 and 1-2 neatly summarize both the good and the bad qualities of supervisors. An effective training program should stress not only the development of positive leadership qualities, but it should also deal with ways to recognize and eliminate negative qualities.

LEADERSHIP GOALS AND SELF-DEVELOPMENT

Security officers who aspire to leadership must continuously grow through self-development. Self-development implies being able to handle increasing responsibility; being able to cope with rapid situational changes; and being able to handle stress. It appears that above all else, attitude has a great bearing upon self-development. A positive attitude is the first step in self-improvement. A

Qualities needed by leaders	How to develop or improve them
Physical and nervous energy	Keep fit Conserve your energy Direct it properly
Sense of purpose and direction	Self-examination: Just where am I headed? What are we trying to do?
Enthusiasm	Maintain vigorous interest Be human—Let yourself go!
Friendliness and understanding (open-mindedness, patience)	Know subordinates personally Be considerate and cordial Develop personality
Integrity (dependability, loyalty)	Be loyal to yourself and your sub- ordinates
Technical skill (knowledge in his field of work)	Constant study, training, and im- provement
Decisiveness (self-confidence)	Get all the facts Make a decision—and act! Be willing to experiment
Intelligence	Don't overestimate your intelligence Obtain the advice of others
Teaching skill	Study teaching methods. Practice teaching
Faith (belief in work or cause)	Do work you can believe in Overcome pessimism

FIGURE 1-1. What makes a leader? Reprinted with permission from *How to Train a Supervisor,* by R. O. Berkman, Harper & Row Publishers Inc., N.Y., 1952.

positive attitude towards the job, the assignment, colleagues, and superiors, and a direct application of what you have learned, will help you achieve your goal. A positive attitude, therefore, is closely linked to self-motivation. If you have a positive attitude, you will be motivated to meet your duties and obligations as an officer and a leader.

Self-improvement requires establishing realistic goals and objectives. These goals and objectives should be readily achievable within a predetermined time frame. Goals should be divided into long-range goals and short-range goals. For example, a long-range goal for a sergeant might be to become a Director of Security within the next five years. The sergeant's short-range goal

Evidences on Supervisor's Part	Effects on Subordinates	Suggestion for Improving
Unfairness Partiality	Will lose respect of favored one. Arouses resentment of others. Slack work.	Give square deal. Put yourself in others' shoes. Treat every man fairly. Play no favorites.
Not practicing what you preach	Contagious. Others will try to get away with it. Disrupts discipline.	Watch your step. Set only good example.
Shirking responsibility "Passing the buck"	Loses respect of superiors and followers. Others begin passing buck. Active dissatisfaction. Disrupts morale.	Shoulder own responsibilities. Take the blame if due. Don't pass the buck.
Not interested in work	Lack of interest on part of men. Poor results.	Get interested or get out!
Over-bearing "High Hat" Unapproachable	Men become "jumpy." Kills initiative. Uneasiness and uncertainty, resentment.	Put yourself in others' shoes. Be human and reasonable.
Quick tempered "Going off half-cocked"	Same as for "over-bearing."	Take time to cool off. Look into various angles before making decision.
Lack of patience	Can't get results. Discourages the men. Afraid to admit they don't understand.	Self-analysis. Work on self-control. Put yourself in others' place. Take time to do job well.
Inconsistent	Men uneasy and unsettled. Hesitate to go ahead. Kills initiative.	Self-analysis. Adopt a uniform policy, and hold to it.
Leader ignorant of job Bluffing	No respect or confidence. Men won't follow lead. Will short-circuit and go to higher-ups for orders.	Apply yourself to learn what you don't know.
Continually finding fault. Nagging.	Kills initiative. Creates ill will.	Be fair. Remember everyone makes mistakes.

FIGURE 1-2. Poor leadership. Reprinted with permission from *How to Train a Supervisor,* by R. O. Berkman, Harper & Row Publishers Inc., N.Y., 1952.

Evidences on Supervisor's Part	Effects on Subordinates	Suggestion for Improving
Leader failure as instructor	Men not properly instructed. Can't perform work properly. Loss of production or property and even life.	Plan your work in advance. Change your methods. Study how to teach.
Unwilling to take suggestions. Won't admit mistakes. Bull-headedness. Conceited.	Kills initiative. Lose benefit of valuable suggestions. Kills cooperation. Men may "frame" leader.	Be open to suggestions at proper time and place. Admit mistakes if occasion arises.
Failure to give credit Grabbing credit where not due	Lack of credit. Resentment. Kills initiative. Stops co-operation.	Put yourself in others' place. Give credit when due.
Lack of consideration for, or interest in, his men.	Crew will lie down on job whenever his back is turned. Men try to put him in hole.	Put yourself in others' place. Be human.
Snooping—"Gumshoe-ing"	Loss of respect. Creates suspicion. Arouses resentment.	Don't do it. Discourage it in others.
Too familiar with men	Loss of respect. Loss of team-work. Loss of discipline.	Maintain a certain reserve befitting position as leader.
Lax discipline	Crew will lie down on job. No team-work. Loss of respect.	Tighten up gradually but firmly and hold for results.
Men lack confidence in him	Won't follow his lead; will wait for orders from higher-ups. No team-work.	Self-analysis. Under certain conditions do job yourself. Actually lead group. Make no promises you can't fill.
Dislike of group for leader	Men will only carry out direct orders. No team-work. Unpleasant feeling.	Check up on self instead. Lead instead of drive. Put self in others' place. Talk over on man-to-man basis. Be courteous and human.
Lack of self-confidence	Men lose confidence in foreman and project.	Assert self. Know what is to be done—and act!

Figure 1-2 continued.

might be to become a lieutenant within the next six months to a year.

To reach the long- and short-range goals it is necessary to convert the goals into measureable and achievable objectives. These objectives should be short, clearly written statements that identify the expected performance outcomes.

Performance objectives fall into four main categories: routine, problem solving, creative, and personal development. These result-oriented statements should indicate what needs to be done and, where appropriate, in what amount of time. Figure 1-3 gives examples of performance objectives typical for security officer duties.

It is conceivable that some outside forces or internal factors will keep you from reaching your immediate or long-range goals. The planning process and the self-development process are not wasted. You will become a better person with your increased knowledge and your added learning experiences.

Your self-development growth may not be immediately apparent nor may your rewards be immediately evident. Perseverance, however, will assist you in reaching your desired objectives. Remember that goals are planned for the future. Without a well-defined road map, you may never reach your final destination. If you establish realistic goals within an achievable time frame, you can accomplish what you set out to do.

Reaching Your Goals

The following general guidelines should help you set up your own leadership development program:

- Seek additional responsibility. If you are comfortable in handling your present duties, and you can assume additional responsibilities, don't hesitate to request them from your superior. It is precisely this type of initiative that placed your boss in the position he now occupies.
- Analyze your immediate situation. Learn from your mistakes and your strengths.
- Learn from others. Identify other people's duties and responsibilities and see if you can use these activities to your best advantage.
- Be realistic in achieving your goals. Your progress toward accomplishment must be possible.
- Constantly evaluate your self-development program. If your situation or opportunities change, your plan may need revision. Evaluate your progress at least every six months to a year. Examine your plan in light of new assignments and don't hesitate to replan your schedule and your goals.

After you establish a goal and estimate the knowledge skills and activities that will be required, the next step is to inventory your assets and your liabil-

Routine objectives

1. Conduct a one-hour in-service training session for security personnel once a month.
2. Conduct a fire drill on a quarterly basis.
3. Monitor all aspects of security operations.
4. Review subordinates' performance quarterly.
5. Conduct routine personnel inspections.
6. Coordinate special orders and assignments during periods of emergency, e.g., bomb threats, fires, etc.

Problem solving objectives

1. Reduce security personnel absenteeism to less than 3%.
2. Improve on-the-job instruction for new officers.
3. Improve security morale.

Personal development

1. Attend at least one professional security workshop/conference.
2. Take a course in management supervision.
3. Read at least five professional security magazine articles a month.
4. Work on improving one weakness identified in my personal inventory list.
5. Begin training a subordinate to take over my assignments so that there will be a replacement available when I get promoted.

FIGURE 1-3.   Performance objectives.

ities. Take the Self Inventory test at the end of this unit. Armed with a personal inventory sheet, you can proceed to acquire knowledge in the areas in which you are deficient. Self-improvement, which requires constant growth, demands understanding and insight on the part of the individual. You must see yourself as others see you. You must identify your strengths and your weaknesses and you must lay out a road map for further development.

Every one has at least two images. One of the images is that which we have of ourselves, the other is the image that everyone else has of us. Ideally, these images should be the same, but they rarely are. Like any other ideal situation, however, considerable effort is needed to make the two agree.

Individuals are what they are because of what they have been or what they have experienced; because of their present circumstances; and because of what they hope to be. There isn't much one can do about the first two items but there is a great deal that can be done about the third.

To a great degree we are what we think we are. "What we think we are" is known as our self-concept. We must take a good look at ourselves before we can engage in any self-improvement. Self-improvement can occur only if you know what needs to be improved.

Once you understand what needs to be improved, you can develop a plan of action. A suggested plan for personality self-improvement is:[2]

[2]Wanat, John A., Brown, John F. and Connin, Lawrence, C., *Hospital Security Guard Training Manual*, Springfield: Charles C. Thomas, 1977, p. 21.

1.   Decide to improve.
2.   Take an initial inventory of habits, attitudes and traits.
3.   Imitate a desired personality by keeping the positive image constantly in your mind.
4.   Work on a single habit or trait at a time until it becomes acceptable, and then proceed to another trait.
5.   Substitute good habits for poor habits and practice the good habits constantly.
6.   Make periodic progress checks and adjust the improvement plan as necessary.

The development of a healthy self-concept involves a long-range project. It is not something that happens overnight. It has to be well thought out and carried out in great detail. In essence, it involves at least a self evaluation; setting realistic goals; a great deal of planning; and it must be achievable.

UNDESIRABLE TRAITS TO BE AVOIDED

The following traits should be avoided at all costs. These traits will prohibit you from improving yourself, not only in your job but in your everyday life. Therefore, avoid them.

- Exploiting people.
- Politicing—currying favors.
- Running people down.
- Being unwilling to change.
- Blaming others for your mistakes.
- Being critical of others.
- Taking credit for ideas or achievements of others.
- Thinking only of yourself. What's in it for me?
- Spreading rumors and gossiping.
- Forcing your ideas and opinions on others.
- Being jealous.
- Making excuses for everything you do.
- Being indifferent to suggestions and criticisms.
- Avoiding or not being able to see other people's point of view.
- Lacking a sense of humor.

Many individuals create personal problems simply because they fail to find out about themselves, their abilities and their objectives. Consequently, self-awareness gains you much.

You can control your negative emotions. It requires that you identify your negative emotions so you can determine how, when and why they occur; and it requires that you identify measures to control these negative emotions.

BROADENING YOUR KNOWLEDGE AND EXPERIENCE

These two tips will help you cultivate positive habits that will lead to self-improvement.

1. Read on a scheduled basis. Self-improvement requires you to be well informed. A regularly scheduled time each day of at least half an hour will be well used if you apply this time to reading. Choose material for reading that will help you grow intellectually and culturally. Your reading material should include security oriented books, magazines and periodicals as well as newspapers and news magazines that will keep you apprised of current events.

2. Seek out formal instruction. Enroll in adult evening programs, community college programs, and college programs that offer subjects in the area you are pursuing. Take every opportunity to attend security association seminars and meetings. Seek out opportunities to participate as a guest lecturer or instructor in subject areas that you are most familiar with. Make it a practice to join discussion groups where you can exchange ideas and opinions. Always remember to maintain an open mind, but be prepared to defend the principles upon which your ideas are based.

LEADERSHIP/SELF IMPROVEMENT CHECK LIST

YES	NO		
☐	☐	1.	I inspire, direct and influence the actions of others.
☐	☐	2.	I have identified my strong and weak points.
☐	☐	3.	I have undertaken a plan to strengthen my weak points.
☐	☐	4.	I endeavor not to be self-centered.
☐	☐	5.	I endeavor to set a good example for my subordinates.
☐	☐	6.	I am attentive to details.
☐	☐	7.	I demonstrate initiative, optimism and enthusiasm.
☐	☐	8.	I constantly strive to improve myself.
☐	☐	9.	I endeavor to develop confidence in myself and in my subordinates.
☐	☐	10.	I keep abreast of current developments in my field.
☐	☐	11.	I take a genuine interest in people.
☐	☐	12.	I listen to what others have to say, weigh their advice and take appropriate and decisive action.
☐	☐	13.	I am fair in my dealings with others.
☐	☐	14.	I keep myself mentally and physically fit.
☐	☐	15.	I assume responsibility for my actions.
☐	☐	16.	I train my subordinates as a team.
☐	☐	17.	I endeavor to give clear and complete instructions.

YES NO

☐ ☐ 18. I set realistic goals.

☐ ☐ 19. I imitate a desired personality.

☐ ☐ 20. I work on one habit or trait at a time until it is acceptable, and then proceed to another trait.

☐ ☐ 21. I substitute good habits for poor habits and practice the good habits constantly.

☐ ☐ 22. I make periodic progress checks and adjust the improvement plan as necessary.

☐ ☐ 23. I am calm and patient under trying times.

☐ ☐ 24. I am tolerant of other people's ideas and customs.

☐ ☐ 25. I exert positive leadership.

☐ ☐ 26. I am generally thoughtful of the feelings of others.

☐ ☐ 27. I am ambitious to get ahead.

☐ ☐ 28. I persevere until I have achieved success.

☐ ☐ 29. I elicit a spirit of cooperation.

☐ ☐ 30. I am free of prejudice.

BIBLIOGRAPHY

American Management Association, *Leadership on the Job, Guides to Good Supervisors*, Selected Readings from *Supervisory Management,* 1966.

Beckman, R.O., *How to Train Supervisors*, Harper & Brothers, New York, 1952.

Bennis, Warren G. and Edgen H. Schiem, eds., *Leadership and Motivation: Essays of Douglas McGregor*, The M.I.T. Press, Massachusetts Institute of Technology, 1966.

"Build the Will to Work", *Nation's Business*, 3rd Edition.

Bureau of Business Practice, *The Standard Manual for Supervisors*, Waterford, Connecticut, 1977.

The Characteristics and Qualities of Leadership Series, Police Reference Notebook, Leadership Resource, Inc., Washington, .D.C.

Department of the Air Force, *Military Management, Air Force Leadership*, Washington, D.C.

Department of the Army, *Military Leadership*, Headquarters, June 1973, FM 22-100.

Department of Education, "Developing a Positive Self Concept: Coordinator's Guide", Tallahassee, Florida.

"Leadership in the Air Force, Extension Course Institute", Gunter Air Force Base, Alabama, 2 B-2.

Petrullo, Luigi and Bernard M. Bass, eds., *Leadership and Interpersonal Behavior*, Holt, Rinehart and Winston, New York, 1961.

Riley, Dr. Clayton and Wendall Bruce, *Personal Development*, Center for Career and Vocational Education, Western Kentucky University, Bowling Green, June, 1974.

United States Jaycees, *Leadership and Action Workbook*, co-sponsored by Massachusetts Mutual Life Insurance Company (25M171), Chapter I, October, 1970.

Vaughn, Paul R., "Personality Pointers", Leadership and Development Series #10, Ohio Association, FFA.

Wanat, John A., John F. Brown and Lawrence C. Connin, *Hospital Security Guard Training Manual*, Charles C. Thomas, Publisher, Springfield, Illinois, Chapter 4, 1977.

2

Motivation and Supervision

The study of motivation is essential in developing supervisory talents. How does a security supervisor establish a climate that will motivate security officers to do their best on the job?

All men are motivated toward something. However, all men do not have the same degree of motivation in all things. Motivation emanates from within the individual. It is personal. The degree of motivation differs from person to person.

A supervisor needs to understand what motivates workers. Once understood, the supervisor should put into practice those factors that will help motivate his subordinates to perform better.

Motivation cannot be forced on an individual. Since motivation stems from within, the supervisor cannot force an employee to be motivated. The supervisor can, however, establish a climate for the employee to become motivated. In order to understand the subject of motivation it is important to understand some motivational theories.

MASLOW'S HIERARCHY OF NEEDS[3]

Abraham H. Maslow theorizes that we are all subject to five sets of basic needs, namely: (1) physiological or survival needs, (2) safety and security needs, (3) affectional or belonging needs, (4) ego or self-esteem needs, and (5) self-fulfillment needs. These needs are hierarchical in nature. That is, they are arranged from lower needs to higher needs. See Figure 2-1.

Physiological or Survival Needs

All men expect immediate satisfaction in regard to meeting their basic physiological survival needs of food, clothing and shelter. A starving person will do whatever is necessary to obtain food for himself and his family. The physiological or survival needs, therefore, are needs that can be satisfied by working to obtain food, clothing and shelter.

---

[3]Maslow, A., *Motivation and Personality*, New York, Harper, 1954.

		(Higher)	
Fifth	Self-Fulfillment Needs		To realize one's potential or goal(s)
Fourth	Ego or Self-Esteem Needs		To achieve status, prestige and self-respect
Third	Social or Belonging Needs		To have an identity, to belong, to be accepted
Second	Safety and Security Needs		To be secure from personal harm; financial security, etc.
First	Physiological or Survival Needs		To satisfy hunger, thirst, etc.
		(Lower)	

FIGURE 2-1.   Maslow's Hierarchy of Needs.

Safety and Security Needs

As the title suggests, safety and security needs include protection from harm or injury. It includes making our lives as safe as possible. However, it goes beyond being protected from physical injury. It includes financial security protection. It means not having to worry about losing your job and the income it provides. It also means reaching and maintaining a standard of living that provides such creature comforts enjoyed by others in society, such as a car, a television, comfortable furniture, entertainment, vacations, a boat, and leisure time.

The first two needs are often referred to as economic needs. The money earned on the job can usually satisfy these needs. Once one is secure in meeting these needs, a higher level need may come into play.

Social or Belonging Needs

This level of need is not as concrete as the other two. Money alone will not satisfy this need. It requires an acceptance by others. It involves affection, love, respect and a sense of belonging from family, friends, colleagues and the groups to which individuals belong. Most people need to relate to others. We need to be noticed, liked and accepted.

Ego or Self-Esteem Needs

This need centers around self-respect, esteem, status and prestige. It means feeling good about ourselves. If we feel good about ourselves we develop a sense of worth about what we do, our ideas, our solutions to problems, and our accomplishments.

Self-Fulfillment Needs

This need heads the hierarchical list. It requires continuous personal growth. It means attaining our full potential or maximizing our abilities to the fullest. It essentially means that you do a good job because you want to and not because you have to.

According to Maslow, you have to satisfy step one, physiological or survival needs, before you can proceed to satisfy step two, safety and security needs. Step two must be satisfied before you proceed to step three, step three before step four, and step four before step five.

Maslow's theory is generally accepted and his hierarchy applies frequently. You should be cautioned, however, against accepting this motivational theory and applying it to all people in all instances. The theory is not absolute. Given unique circumstances and individual differences, the hierarchical order may not apply.

THE MOTIVATION HYGIENE THEORY OF FREDERICK HERZBERG[4]

According to Frederick Herzberg, there are two separate processes of motivation, namely: motivation factors and hygiene factors. The motivation factors are those that satisfy when reached. The hygiene factors are those that do not truly satisfy when reached, but *do* dissatisfy when not obtained. Each process will be discussed in detail.

Motivation Factors

Herzberg's motivation factors deal primarily with the job itself. This portion of his theory is essentially founded in job satisfaction and the opportunities which cause motivation. The factors that act as motivators in job satisfaction are identified as achievement, recognition, challenge, responsibility and growth.

Supervisors must be aware of what subordinates expect from an employment situation. Failure to understand workers' expectations can result in dissatisfied and unmotivated workers.

[4]Herzberg, Frederick, *Work and the Nature of Man*, Cleveland: World, 1966 and Herzberg, Frederick et al., *The Motivation to Work*, New York: Wiley, 1959.

Achievement

Supervisors must set attainable goals that can be met by their subordinates. Help instill the feeling in subordinates that they can succeed if they try.

Recognition

Give credit when credit is due. A supervisor should praise subordinates for a job well done. A security officer who constantly performs well but who is not recognized for his work may become dissatisfied.

Give your surbordinates the recognition they want, need, and deserve.

Challenge

Subordinates should be given the opportunity to do new and more difficult tasks.

Responsibility

Let subordinates feel important to the organization. Supervisors should delegate assignments and responsibility to subordinates whenever possible. A delegated assignment should never be given without also delegating the responsibility to carry out the assignment. The responsibility should include freedom to act within established procedures and in accordance with company policy.

Growth

Make opportunities available for subordinates to grow on the job. Supervisors should arrange for in-service training, attending professional, seminars, and challenging tasks.

Whenever possible, supervisors should recommend promotion from within. Individuals who do a good job and can handle responsibility should be given the opportunity to advance. Employees are concerned about their future. People will often take a lower paying job if they feel that opportunities are good for advancement.

Peoples' actions are geared to satisfy their needs. After meeting their basic survival needs, job satisfaction ranks high on most employees' list of needs. If employees are not satisfied, it is nearly impossible for them to become motivated.

The best technique a security supervisor can take to inspire motivation in his subordinates is to provide challenging work that requires the individual to exercise authority and responsibility. This technique should be used at every level of the organizational structure. The security supervisor should assign tasks, provide the necessary guidance and then hold the security officer responsible for its accomplishment.

The adages "Achievement is its own best reward," and "Nothing succeeds like success," are statements that should be put into practice. Most individuals want to be given a challenging task. They need the authority to carry out the assignment, and the flexibility, within company guidelines and policies, to bring the assignment to a successful conclusion.

It is also very important for the supervisor to recognize a job well done and say so to the subordinate. The earned recognition will motivate the subordinate to even greater heights. In addition, the esteem and self-realization of a job well done will provide further motivation.

Hygiene Factors

Herzberg's hygiene factors focus on the job surroundings. They deal with those things which, if not present or if inadequate, cause job dissatisfaction. For example, acquiring money is a drive for people who are seeking to satisfy their basic needs of food, clothing and shelter. It continues to be a drive for many who are seeking the comforts enjoyed by their peers.

Money or pay, for many people, become less of a drive as basic wants and needs are satisfied. Pay in itself is usually not a motivator. It rarely, if ever, provides job satisfaction. However, the absence of an increase in pay can be a dissatisfier.

Reduction in pay, or a failure to get a raise or cost of living increase, will result in poor morale. For the most part, people are more concerned about being paid fairly than they are about being paid large sums of money.

Herzberg holds that poor pay, low social status, poor working conditions, or intolerable interpersonal relations are "dissatisfiers." Any one of these factors can cause the security officers to perform poorly. In all probability, they will be so concerned with their own well-being that they will exclude all activities which do not lead to this satisfaction.

People's actions are based on their desire to satisfy their needs. How well they will perform depends to a great extent on how satisfied they are with the job, and how motivated they are to perform well. The average security officer will be dissatisfied on the job if his needs of security, salary, status, work conditions or interpersonal relations are not met.

Dissatisfiers

Factors that tend to dissatisfy subordinates are:

- Excessive work rules
- Demonstrating favoritism
- Poor wages
- Lack of coffee and smoke breaks
- Poor fringe benefits
- Inappropriate job titles
- Poor working conditions
- Overbearing supervision

Eliminating dissatisfiers will not, in and of itself, motivate subordinates. It will, however, provide the climate in which subordinates can be motivated.

MAINTENANCE NEEDS

During the 1960s, Texas Instruments, Inc. conducted an exhaustive study on motivation. Based on that study, M. Scott Myers wrote an article entitled "Who Are Your Motivated Workers?" The author stated, "The supervisor's role is twofold. He must:

1. Provide conditions of motivation.
2. Satisfy maintenance needs."

Maintenance needs are:

- *Economic*—wages and salaries, automatic increases, profit sharing, social security, workmen's compensation, unemployment compensation, retirement, paid leave, insurance, tuition, discounts
- *Security*—fairness, consistency, reassurance, friendliness, seniority rights, grievance procedures
- *Orientation*—job instruction, work rules, group meetings, shop talk, newspapers, bulletins, handbooks, letters, bulletin boards, grapevine
- *Status*—job classification, title, furnishings, location, privileges, relationships, company status
- *Social*—work groups, coffee groups, lunch groups, social groups, office parties, ride pools, outings, sports, professional groups, interest groups
- *Physical*—work layout, job demands, work rules, equipment, location, grounds, parking facilities, aesthetics, lunch facilities, rest rooms, temperature, ventilation, lighting, noise[5]

MOTIVATIONAL TECHNIQUES

E.I. Du Pont De Nemours and Company lists the following factors in their information brochure as being important to the morale and motivation of its employees:

1. Have concern for the individual.
2. Treat the employee as an individual rather than just as a member of a group.

[5]Meyers, M. Scott, "Who are Your Motivated Workers?" January/February 1964, *Harvard Business Review*, 1964. Reproduced with permission by the President and Fellows of Harvard College. All rights reserved.

3.   Promote from within whenever feasible.
4.   Assign tasks that enable the individual to practice his skills, to discover his own strengths and weaknesses, and ultimately to bid for opportunities in those areas where he can make a satisfying contribution.[6]

THEORY X AND THEORY Y[7]

Douglas McGregor made a major contribution to the study of motivation by advancing two theories about human behavior—Theory X and Theory Y. The theories have two distinct and contrasting philosophies.

Theory X advocates a classical belief that individuals have an inherent dislike for work and that they will do whatever they can to avoid it. Those who uphold this theory believe that the average person wants to be directed, avoids responsibility and has very little drive.

Theory Y, on the other hand, advocates that the average person is self-directed and is self-controlled.

This theory supports the concept that people will and do seek out increased responsibility. Work, to those who adhere to the Theory Y concept, is as natural as rest and relaxation.

A wise supervisor will try to understand the individuals who work for him. Some subordinates may fall into the Theory X category. They may need more direction and control than others. Those subordinates who fit the Theory Y category should be given the opportunity to engage in self-destruction and self-control to reach their objectives and goals. Unquestionably, individuals who fall into the latter category need less direction than those in the former category. The key to utilizing the Theory X and Theory Y concept is to assess each subordinate to try to understand what motivates them.

There is no one answer or secret to motivating others. Since human beings are all very different and since they have different motives for doing things, it is then the responsibility of the supervisor to try to understand what motivates each and every one of his subordinates. Only then can he effectively motivate others to do their job better.

MAINTAINING A SECURITY SYSTEM

Motivation is, perhaps, the most important skill a supervisor needs to develop, but there are others which are necessary to the effective operation of a security organization. A supervisor, being part of the management team, is the essential

---

[6] "The Organization and the Individual," *This is Du Pont,* #26, E.I. Du Pont De Nemours and Company, Wilmington, Delaware, 1964, pp. 15 and 30.

[7] McGregor, Douglas, *The Human Side of Enterprise* (New York: McGraw-Hill 1960).

link between top management and the line officers. They are action-oriented individuals who must interpret and implement security policy.

The security supervisor is responsible for maintaining a security system that accomplishes the following:[8]

1.   The protection of life and property
2.   The preservation of the peace
3.   The prevention of vandalism and other crimes
4.   The prevention and detection of fire and safety hazards
5.   The enforcement of security rules and regulations

Protection of Life and Property involves, but is not limited to, conducting periodic security tours, both internal and external; providing escort service for personnel during late evening hours; and establishing 24-hour-a-day security coverage.

Preservation of the Peace includes the restraint and/or removal of disorderly persons; crowd control; and maintaining order.

Prevention of Vandalism and other Crimes includes maintaining security posts, watching for anything out of the ordinary, being available to provide assistance when needed. Good patrolling is one of the keys to the prevention of vandalism and other crimes.

Prevention and Detection of Fire and Safety Hazards includes watch clock tours—fire checks, adherence to all fire and safety regulations. Staff training is essential.

Enforcement of Security Rules and Regulations includes visitor pass control and enforcement of company security policies in general.

DUTIES OF A SECURITY SUPERVISOR

"A supervisor is a supervisor is a supervisor," regardless of what area the supervisor is assigned. The degree and frequency of some duties may vary from one job to another, but essentially supervisors perform the same tasks. These tasks are numerous, complex, and varied. They also demand a great deal of the supervisor's time, planning ability, and organizational ability. Following are brief descriptions of supervisory duties. More specific supervisory duties are listed in Figure 2-2.

Managerial

A supervisor is responsible for directing the personnel and operations under his

[8]Wanat, John A., Brown, John F., and Connin, Lawrence C. *Hospital Security Guard Training Manual*, Springfield, Thomas, 1977, pg. 6.

Personnel

- Assists in selection of security personnel
- Recommends security officers for promotion and merit awards
- Conducts security force discipline
- Enforces rules and regulations
- Conducts security personnel inspections
- Conducts field supervision
- Administers employee identification system
- Issues and enforces employee parking

Interacts with Visitors

- Establishes and enforces visitor control procedures
- Establishes and enforces vendor control procedures
- Regulates parking and traffic control
- Enforces package pass regulations

Training

- Provides on-the-job training to new, as well as to experienced, security officers
- Conducts formal lectures and classes on a wide range of security topics to security personnel as well as to other company employees
- Demonstrates proper procedures in a wide range of safety and security areas, such as: fire extinguishment and evacuation; bomb search; patrol functions; establishing emergency and disaster control centers; handling mob activities, strikes and pickets
- Arranges for personnel to attend outside lectures, classes, seminars, conventions and professional security activities

Interacts with other Professionals

- Liaison with law enforcement
- Liaison with government safety agencies
- Liaison with fire department
- Liaison with military and police bomb disposal unit
- Liaison with First Aid/paramedic units
- Liaison with other security professionals

FIGURE 2-2. Specific security supervisory duties.

control. This function requires the supervisor to plan, organize and control the work of others. It includes implementing company policies, setting standards and goals, establishing priorities, and coordinating team efforts.

Communications

The supervisor has to keep the lines of communication open at all levels. Both staff and management must be kept informed of all essential operational and policy matters. Communication responsibilities include: preparing reports required by management; reporting progress, problems and solutions; maintaining records; conducting data analysis on accidents; and circulating incident reports.

Budgeting

Security operations require financial resources to hire and maintain security personnel and support staff as well as to acquire, maintain and update equipment and supplies. The supervisor, therefore, assists in preparing operational budgets and forecasts. After the budgets are approved and authorized, the supervisor must justify expenditures, approve supply requests and overtime operations, and maintain inventory and payroll records.

Operational

The supervisor's operational duties account for most of his or her working time. It includes, but is not limited to: planning and organizing workloads; delegating assignments; troubleshooting problems; handling staffing problems, including making decisions on hiring, firing and recommending promotions; providing technical assistance, and coordinating on-the-job activities.

Control

The supervisor has to establish and maintain quality standards of operation. In this regard he has to: enforce company regulations; take corrective action when needed; conduct safety and security inspections; maintain order and discipline; evaluate performance.

IMPROVING SUPERVISION SKILLS

Security policies are only as effective as the supervisors who implement them. Supervisors can make the difference between achievement and failure by the way they work with people, give job assignments, and provide leadership. A supervisor should know how to:

- Organize the work to be done, plan it as far ahead as possible, and break it down into its parts
- Delegate fairly to employees the tasks best suited to them
- Coordinate the work of your unit with the company's total operations
- Maintain composure and leadership in the face of changed policies, superimposed regulations, or lack of materials, equipment, and facilities

- Be able to get along with good people who may be very different from each other, getting them to work together willingly and efficiently.[9]

Supervisors have to be people oriented. They must know how to work with people, delegate assignments, generate results and provide leadership and training. Furthermore, supervisors must be skilled in communication, human relations, management skills, safety awareness and company policies. Above all, supervisors must have leadership ability.

Security supervisors are frequently promoted from the ranks. Consequently, they usually have to develop and/or improve their supervisory skills. Although there is no great mystery to the art of supervision, there are a few useful techniques that supervisors can adopt that will make their job rewarding and productive.

- Be up-to-date on technical techniques in security
- Be responsive to suggestions and new ideas
- Be fair in dealing with subordinates
- Be thoroughly familiar with company policy and operational procedures
- Be willing to delegate authority and responsibility
- Be able to effectively communicate up and down the chain of command
- Be supportive of staff
- Be skillful in promoting good community relations
- Be willing to give credit where credit is due
- Be willing to listen with an open ear
- Be prepared to train subordinates

DEVELOPING SUBORDINATE'S TALENTS

As action-oriented individuals, security supervisors must rely on the talents of others. Simply delegating assignments to others, however, is not enough. Supervisors must first identify officers' talents, cultivate their talents, and then delegate responsibilities that maximize these talents.

Effective security supervisors are wise enough to realize that their jobs can be impossible if officers are not fully qualified to handle their assignments and responsibilities. Supervisors should, therefore, develop their officers' talents to the utmost.

In developing officers' talents, supervisors should:

- Provide, where possible, challenging assignments. Not all security assignments can be challenging. Some are routine, and some are even boring. You might not be able to make all assignments challenging. However, you can stress the importance of the assignment as it relates to the total security function.

[9]*Developing Your Manpower*, United States Department of Labor, Manpower Administration, U.S. Government Printing Office, Washington, D.C. 1970, pg. 11.

- Clarify company policy and regulations. All too often, officers, too, do not know why company policies and regulations are enacted. By keeping security officers informed you will probably keep them from coming up with erroneous reasons for company actions.
- Provide clear instructions as to what is to be done, what method or procedure is to be followed, and what deadline is to be met.
- Demonstrate the proper procedures. Don't assume that your security officers understand how to perform an operation, e.g., handle a CO_2 fire extinguisher. The best way to insure the proper procedure is to demonstrate or provide detailed instructions.
- Answer questions willingly. Be straightforward and honest. There are times when you can't or shouldn't reveal some information. In that case say that you are not at liberty to discuss the issue.
- Supervise the security officers' performance on-the-job. Most officers want to know how their supervisor perceives their performance. It indicates to them that you are concerned and interested in them as individuals and as officers.
- Provide the security officer with a regularly scheduled, fair, and honest evaluation of his work performance. Set aside the time to conduct this important supervisory function. If you use this time wisely, you can assist officers to overcome shortcomings, while reinforcing their strong points.
- Recommend security officers for promotion based on objective evaluations of their performance. Don't allow your personal bias to overrule your sound judgement.
- Provide routine in-service training sessions. Don't forget to solicit feedback from your officers on their training needs as well as the training rendered.
- Make provisions for security officers to attend outside training sessions, workshops, conferences and meetings.

SUPERVISORY PITFALLS

Frequently supervisors get caught in "binds" because they failed to adhere to some basic principles. Supervision requires a great deal of introspection on the part of the supervisor. A wise supervisor will set aside time to review his accomplishments, successes and failures.

We all make mistakes at times. A good supervisor learns from his mistakes and, if possible, does not repeat them a second time. Listed below are some common pitfalls for supervisors.

- Failure to properly delegate responsibility
- Failure to effectively communicate instructions
- Failure to allow subordinates to exercise initiative
- Failure to keep subordinates informed
- Failure to weigh the facts before making decisions

- Failure to maintain quality standards
- Failure to define responsibilities
- Failure to clarify company policy and procedures
- Failure to conduct line inspections
- Failure to provide in-service training
- Failure to set a good example
- Failure to identify subordinates' strengths
- Failure to practice effective human relations

SELF INVENTORY CHECKLIST

YES	NO		
☐	☐	1.	I endeavor to keep my staff informed and up to date on all company policies and procedures.
☐	☐	2.	I effectively delegate assignments to subordinates that are best suited to them.
☐	☐	3.	I spell out each subordinate's authority and responsibility.
☐	☐	4.	I avail myself to subordinates for technical assistance.
☐	☐	5.	I maximize the use of my subordinate's talents.
☐	☐	6.	I encourage subordinates to be creative.
☐	☐	7.	I organize my work in an orderly fashion.
☐	☐	8.	I endeavor to set a good example for my subordinates.
☐	☐	9.	I set realistic standards and appropriate time tables to reach the desired objectives.
☐	☐	10.	I get all the facts on gripes and complaints.
☐	☐	11.	I handle grievances promptly and fairly.
☐	☐	12.	I weight all facts before making a decision.
☐	☐	13.	I provide my subordinates with a challenge.
☐	☐	14.	I train subordinates to "fill my shoes."
☐	☐	15.	I effectively communicate up and down the chain of command.
☐	☐	16.	I provide personalized attention to my subordinates.
☐	☐	17.	I praise colleagues for doing a good job.
☐	☐	18.	I avoid disagreement and conflict whenever possible.
☐	☐	19.	I encourage employees to suggest improvements.
☐	☐	20.	I treat my employees as individuals.
☐	☐	21.	I keep subordinates informed about their progress.
☐	☐	22.	I know my subordinates' capabilities.
☐	☐	23.	I endeavor to establish challenging attainable goals.
☐	☐	24.	I give credit when credit is due.
☐	☐	25.	I keep my subordinates informed on how their duties contribute to the entire operation.
☐	☐	26.	I establish a climate for employees to become motivated.
☐	☐	27.	I understand what motivates workers.

YES NO

☐   ☐   28. I endeavor to promote from within.
☐   ☐   29. I encourage my subordinates to keep trying until they succeed.
☐   ☐   30. I provide my subordinates with opportunities to grow on the job.

BIBLIOGRAPHY

Burnstein, Harvey: "You Are Management," *Industrial Security*, 5: 18, January, 1961.

Davis, James A.: "What is a Security Director?", *Industrial Security*, December, 1970.

"Developing Your Manpower," United States Department of Labor, Manpower Administration, U.S. Government Printing Office, Washington, D.C., 1970.

Gellerman, Saul: *Motivation and Productivity*, American Management Association, New York, 1963.

Healy, Richard J.: "Putting Security on The Management Team," *Security World*, 2, No. 5: July - August, 1965.

Herzberg, Frederick, "One More Time: How Do You Motivate Employees?" *Harvard Business Review*, January - February, 1968, pp. 53-62.

Herzberg, Frederick, et al.: *The Motivation to Work*, New York, Wiley, 1959.

Herzberg Frederick: *Work and The Nature of Man*, Cleveland: World, 1966.

Leadership in The Air Force, Extension Course Institute, Air University, Alabama, Course 2B.

Maslow, Abraham H.: *Motivation and Personality*, New York, Harper, 1954.

Mason, G. Joseph, *How to Build Management Skills,* McGraw-Hill, 1965.

"Motivation," *Military Leadership,* Headquarters, Department of the Army, FM 22-100, June, 1973, pp. 8-1/6-8.

McGregor, Douglas: *The Human Side of Enterprise*, McGraw Hill, New York, 1960.

Motivation—No Substitute For The Human Touch, Supervisor's bulletin . . . for line and staff. Bureau of Business Practices, Inc., April 30, 1978, #540, pp. 1-3.

Motivation, The Supervisor's Problem-Solving Series, Bureau of Business Practices, Waterford, Conn., July, 1970, #104.

Myers, M. Scott, *Who Are Your Motivated Workers? How Successful Executives Handle People*, 12 Studies on Communications and Management Skill, Harvard Business Review, 1964, pp. 73-88.

Post, Richard S. and Kingsbury, Arthur A.: *Security Administration, An Introduction*, 3rd Ed. Springfield, Thomas, 1977.

Steeno, David L., "Give Your People The Opportunity to Fail: A Reply," *Security Management,* Vol. 23, No. 9, September 1979, pp. 114-118.

"The Organization and The Individual," *This is Du Pont,* #26, E.I. Du Pont De Nemours and Company, Wilmington, Delaware, 1964, pp. 15 and 30.

The Standard Manual for Supervisors, Bureau of Business Practice, Waterford, Connecticut, 1969.

Wanat, John A., Brown, John F., Connin, Lawrence C.: *Hospital Security Guard Training Manual*, Charles C. Thomas, Publisher, Springfield, Illinois, 1977.

3

Management and the Management Functions

The success of any business endeavor—whether your role is that of employee, employer or proprietor—is directly related to your management skills. While effective business practices, through the development of management skills, do not guarantee successful operations, they do lessen the odds of failure considerably.

The executive officers who combine to form the "Administration" level are responsible for security, which, in most industrial situations, is an essential and specialized management function. If they fail to oversee the institution of terms of promoting and supporting the security program, they will suffer from their negligence.

Administration has a seemingly unending list of expectations for the security director, for the security supervisors, and the security department. From a negative viewpoint, many companies want FBI service at the minimum wage, as opposed to a good, reliable support service. They are often crisis-oriented and react to accidents, disasters, energy shortages, strikes and other labor confrontations. You should have your emergency plans ready, by establishing and continually updating your files with new equipment, theories, and methods. By doing so, you are practicing good management techniques.

The executive suite wants the Department of Security to plan, control, organize, direct and have concern. Obviously, they desire effective managers in all departments. Basically, this involves common sense, honesty, dependability and continually developing sound management skills.

Management has the responsibility of providing the maximum product or service to their consumers at a reasonable cost. Proper security eliminates unnecessary expense by minimizing loss.

Management is defined as the "art, act, or manner of managing, controlling, and directing." It is getting work done through people—preferably both effectively and efficiently. These two terms, although they are close in definition, are not identical in meaning. Peter Drucker writes that *efficiency* is doing better than that which is already being done, with a focus on costs. *Effectiveness,* the more desired result, focuses on the best way to produce extraordinary results. But they must go hand in hand to assure survival. Effectiveness is the foundation for success, while efficiency is an aid to survival after success has been attained.

"Efficiency is concerned with doing things right. Effectiveness is doing the right things."[10]

Your administration wants you first to be a manager—one who is able to communicate and cooperate. But don't be just a manager—be an effective manager!

As Keith MacKeller, the president of the International Association for Hospital Security, said several years ago, "one of the greatest problems facing hospitals today is not internal theft, not drug abuse, not employee relations,, not tight financial situations...it is the inability of many security directors to function on a managment level!" The statement appears to be still valid and it applies to all fields of security. We will continue to emphasize that security is first a management function, not a police function!

MANAGEMENT QUALITIES

The management qualities of the security director must certainly include keeping a positive image, managing time effectively, and learning to deal with people. Security is only unique in its responsibilities for protection and its activities in prevention. Your staff has to master techniques of understanding and handling people. They have to be people-oriented.

Security executives should also have expertise in several areas, including personnel policies and procedures, labor relations, OSHA regulations, and the laws of arrest. Security executives often find themselves functioning as attorney, psychologist, clergyman, policeman, public relations consultant, confidential advisor, friend, and as a marketing specialist promoting their programs.

PLANNING

Planning is an integral function of a manager. A manager plans in order to know where his department has come from, where it is now, and where it is going. He must look into a crystal ball for the future, set up some service goals, and map a trail from the present point to the desired point considering the identified goals. Using additional judgment, the manager then evaluates the plan by using it as a measuring rod to determine if the course is accurate. If off-course, the direction must be reset and tracked more closely.

A plan is used as a policy guide for key decisions, a framework of operations, and a statement of role and future intentions to administration, other departments and interested parties.

Planning becomes more important today due to the growth of industries, competition, technological and social trends. The vital factors in goal setting are forecasting accurately and on a timely basis.

[10]Peter F. Drucker, *Management: Tasks, Responsibilities, Practices.* New York: Harper & Row, 1974, p. 45.

The manager must first decide what needs to be done. It is important to set short- and long-range objectives for the organization, and to decide on the means that will be used to meet them. In order to.do this, you must forecast the economic, social and political environment in which the organization will be operating, and the resources it will have available to make the plans work out. Plans that are entirely feasible in a time of prosperity may be utterly impractical in a period of depression. Planning may be said to encompass budgeting, since a budget is a plan to spend a certain amount of money to accomplish certain objectives.

All goals that are set must be defined. Establish what you want to do and what you should do. These are called objectives. Thereafter, list various alternative courses of action. Finally, list the selected courses of action, tell what you are going to do. However, be sure to include contingency plans.

Decide on the means to accomplish the objectives, often called programming, within the limits of available resources.

Assemble data to compare the planned goals and objectives with past performance. Your requirements for personnel, equipment, and materials must be analyzed and projected.

The Daily Report

A basic source of data is the security officers' Daily Report which is a running log of activities. It is recommended that a compilation of these reports, called "Daily Shift Report" or "Security Supervisors' Report," also be submitted to the security administrator. This latter report becomes the basis for monthly and yearly reports, and serves as an aid to ascertain personnel and equipment requirements.

The "Daily Shift Report" may include: staffing, assistance rendered, complaints, concern services, vehicle mileage and usage, watchlock tours, incidents and accidents, doors unlocked and doors found unlocked, interviews, inspections, alarms, property passes, lost and found property, calls to police/fire department, V.I.P. visitors, supplies needed, equipment defects, and other noteworthy occurances.

The data base, or information base, can then be collected on an organized basis and statistical reports and graphs can illustrate your activities, your problems, and your proposed solutions. A computer can facilitate storing, accessing, and updating of the data.

Your program must be planned step by step, with reasonable goals. Often, managers will cite immediate goals in order to achieve some level of accomplishment. This may stimulate establishing and accomplishing longer range goals. Time tables should be set to guide action and serve as challenges.

Effective lines of communications must be established, and most importantly, any key people who are affected or involved in your plan must be convinced to accept it. This last step is generally referred to as "playing politics."

Finally, do not procrastinate. Take some action, because you must! And thereafter, enjoy the satisfaction of accomplishment.

OBSTACLES TO PLANNING

Managers do not always accept being commited to definite goals within specified time periods. Often, they are preoccupied with day-to-day activities and "crises." Planning must include realistic goals and managers must be convinced that proposed solutions will reduce the chance of a "crisis" and save time.

Managers sometimes get turned-off by the impossible task of forecasting. However, they must be convinced that "guesstimates" are better than no forecasting at all.

People, by nature, are suspicious of, and resist, change. Goals, objectives, courses of action, and sometimes entire plans must be changed. Being realistic in your initial planning efforts will minimize great changes. This should reduce frustrations.

Some of these obstacles may include your own reasons for resisting plans and planning. You, and other managers, must fully understand the purpose and importance of a plan. The solution to these obstacles is a complete and clear understanding before the planning process is initiated.

PLANNING AND THE BUDGET

The first departmental planning effort is usually the budget. Ideally, the security department submits its own budget and does not have it tied to another department's. The security department should prepare and stand alone in its budgets, annual reports, monthly activity and progress reports.

The budget is a vital tool for communication. Once it is written and approved, it becomes a binding expression of established policies, goals and objectives, and commits the means for attaining those goals and objectives. A budget is not just a list of figures estimating your requirements for the next year. A budget becomes a standard to measure your performance and effectiveness. Thereafter, a budget assists in establishing priorities since the limited resources must be controlled and used sparingly. With that thought in mind, include some suggestions for cost containment and cost reduction in your budget. Justify all your costs, since you are vying with other managers for funds.

Make your recommendations if you believe in them even if they are costly. You should provide alternatives and explain the obvious effect of providing a lesser degree of security. But let administration decide where compromises are to be made. The Golden Rule of the Arts and Science is, "Whoever has the gold, makes the rules." (Book of Lists, 481). But also remember "Faint heart never won fair lady.'' Sell the benefits of equipment, such as CCTV, that will cut manpower costs. Forecast expected lifetime value to demonstrate how it will effectively offset the initial cost. Use Cost Analysis Methods of Comparison.

One very important warning: don't overbudget! Dollars are usually limited. You must account rigidly for all expenditures, and demonstrate benefits to the company. Don't fabricate your budget and ask for three people when you know that you'll get cut a cut and wind up with one and a half which is what you actually required. The suspicion of ''puffery'' will always be attached to you.

Be prepared to identify and justify how last year's allotment was expended. Promote positive aspects and favorable results. For example, as a result of using the CCTV, a theft was discovered and lead to the apprehension of X employees and the recovery of *$XX.* Also report that the investment of monies for training resulted in a professional staff. Indicate several instances, and don't be shy.

Don't wait to submit a budget to state your case for your needs. Keep upper management informed continually of what you are doing, and what your problems are, through monthly activity and progress reports, as well as annual reports. The assumption is that when top management knows about your unresolved problems or deficiencies, they will be more inclined to approved your budget.

Sample Budget Outline

ABC International
Security Department
Budget 1980

Narrative Report

I. *Major Accomplishments*
    What did you do since the last budget that you are proud of, or believe that upper management should be aware of. If you accomplish something with the aid of additional monies from your last year's budget, say so!

II. *Personnel*
    Include current staffing and projected needs for next year. Justify any requested new positions. Discuss quality of staff candidly and include recommendations for improving the security department through training programs, equipment, etc.

III. *Comparative Analysis*
    Use your statistical data to reflect your department's activity, to identify problem areas, and to indicate corrective action.

IV.　*Unresolved Problems*
Mention them again (but don't be sarcastic).

V.　*Capital Equipment Requirements*
Cite needed items, justify their purchase to provide additional mechanical support of your Security efforts. It is also very important to continually plan to replace equipment as it becomes ineffective. A suggested three-year phasing might include:

> 1981:　4 Walkie-Talkies (2 replacements)
> 1982:　4 Walkie-Talkies (3 replacements)
> 1983:　3 Walkie-Talkies (all replacements)

VI.　*Projections for the Future*
Cite both long-range and short-range goals, and your objectives. Also cite cost savings or cost avoidance.

VII.　*Comment*
This section allows you the opportunity to thank others for their acceptance and support of you, your staff and your program.

Respectfully submitted,

John R. Jones
Security Supervisor

Attached to the narrative report, you should detail the breakdown of each cost center and include the following, for the subject year only:

Salaries
Total with all anticipated raises and contingent overtime forecast

Supplies and Expenses
Office Supplies
Printing
Film and Processing
Telephone/Postage

Education, Training and Travel
Seminars and Meetings
Membership
Books, Magazines and Training Aids

Capital Equipment
(This year only)

Rental of Equipment (or leasing)
  (This year only)

Fees
  Special coverage by additional Officers/Police or contract guard agency

Maintenance
  Equipment
  Uniforms
  Other

Miscellaneous
  Any unique requirements that do not fit comfortably in the above
  categories.

Remember, you must recognize the limitations of any plan or budget. You
are basing projections on estimates and they, of course, are not always
predictable.

PRINCIPLES OF ORGANIZATION

The security department must be structured around the needs of the organization. Your security plan, definitions of responsibility, policies, and procedures
must be established. Author Russ Colling, has long promoted the idea that,
"We are here to support you—not to interfere with operations." A suitable
message might be: we are not playing cops and robbers; our emphasis is on prevention not apprehension; and we strive to contribute to the end product of our
organization. Again, the key is management.
    Organizing establishes an orderly arrangement of personnel, equipment,
and material to effectively facilitate achieving the organization's objectives.
    Every manager is responsible for the business enterprise and for contrib-
uting to its successful operation. He must effectively use manpower, facilities,
equipment, and material, and must effectively coordinate and cooperate with
other managers and departments throughout the organization.
    Your first step in organizing is to ascertain the attitude of your own super-
visor toward security. Thereafter, establish your responsibilities and authority.
Clarify any gray areas and define your security program. The limitations of
authority must be delineated. The chain of command has to be clear from the
administrator, through you the supervisor, to the patrolling security officer. You
are responsible for the effective implementation of your assigned tasks and your
security program as adopted by the administration.
    The second step is to determine the needs of your facility and mold your

department and your protective interests into the organization. The location usually determines the type of security required. An urban industry will depend heavily on police force techniques, while a suburban one will have more emphasis on public relations.

Your product/service and its potential for theft or damage must also be considered in establishing your necessary style of protection. Decisions on armed officers, nightsticks, uniforms or blazers, and mandatory employee bonding will then have to be made. Other considerations include your building design, and the type of employees present. Both will have a great effect on your decisions. The following concepts are considered to be universally applicable to all organizations.

1. *Division of Work*—Work must be divided into areas of responsibility that are clearly defined. Related tasks are then grouped and their responsibility is assigned to one supervisor and the work is delegated to a predetermined group of employees.

2. *Definition of Tasks and Functions*—A clear and complete understanding of tasks and functions must be provided in writing to insure effective performance.

3. *Authority and Responsibility*—Responsibility for various tasks and functions will be assigned by the chief executive officer to subordinates. It is fixed by assignment and defined for clarification. A manager must have the authority delegated before he can be responsible to carry any task or function out.

4. *Span of Control*—A supervisor cannot control, direct, and otherwise coordinate an excessive number of employees as subordinates. No more than 8-10 employees is often recommended for effective supervision and a workable span of control.

5. *Unity of Command*—Simply stated, each department, shift, and employee should be under the control of only *one* person at a time.

6. *Authority and Communication*—Lines of authority must be properly defined and the lines of communication for directions and information must be explained. An organizational chart is recommended for your own security department, which will map the flow of communications up, down, and laterally.

Reorganizing the Department

It may be time for you to rethink your department's philosophy, objectives, and methods. You have already analyzed your administrator. Now it's time for you to determine the style and quality of your department, your staff, and yourself. After evaulation, you will have determined needs, equipment, and personnel. Now set your priorities and allocate your resources in those areas.

If appropriate, restructure your department. Use participative management where possible. Delegate responsibility to the security supervisors with only major matters referred back to you for decision. If your staff is not responsible, develop them, transfer them, or dismiss them. Be "operations oriented" toward effective and efficient compliance with management policies and procedures.

If you are the senior officer in your security department, and you are still in uniform, with the title of Captain or Chief, you might want to start reorganizing here. Convert to an executive image with a suite and tie, and a proper title of Director of Security or Security Administrator. The act of getting out of a uniform may lead to your acceptance by the other department heads as a fellow member of the management team.

You might consider proposing expanding the concept and authority of security to that of Loss Prevention Services or Risk Management. Compatible activities might include: safety, fire prevention, OSHA, Workmen's Compensation, insurance, transportation, and possibly communications.

Again, on a personal note, consider rewriting your job description—update it to include your additional experience and education. Back to an organizational level, develop and propose changing the appropriate administrative policies and procedures. Promote awareness by others that management input from the security department is vital.

Since we no longer wish to identify with "fat cops stealing apples" or "night watchmen doing rounds between naps and nips," protective services must be implemented by a corps of trained professionals interfacing with the entire management team. Your goals, again, must be coordinated with your organization's primary goals.

The security force must be visible, not low-keyed. Put in an extra watch clock tour so that the staff sees the security officers more than they want to. At night or during off-hours, have them stop at each work station and ask if everything is O.K. They can even be required to record the name of who they spoke to and at what time. There is no need, of course, for a coffee klatch meeting, but this friendly tour will insure that no one can say that security is never around.

STAFFING

Staffing is the actual hiring of the right person to fill each of the positions that have been created in the organization. It encompasses recruiting, selecting, training, promoting, and transferring. However, before any of these functions are initiated, a management decision must be made, and quite possibly it must be made by you. That decision is whether that new position should be created. Should an additional security officer be budgeted or should you simply adjust your schedule, or provide overtime for your current staff? The staffing functions are continuing exercises because the firm's and your own department's plans and objectives frequently necessitate changes in organization.

A security manager's staffing responsibilities, particularly the training aspect, appears to be one without end. Training, in its every mode, must be a continuing program for all security personnel. As previously mentioned, in the discussion of reorganizing, if your staff is not responsible you must develop them or dismiss them.

Training materials to assist you are widely available today and the importance of training is certainly a recurring theme throughout this book. But two options, training or dismissing, should be considered at this time. Training is the easiest alternative, and considering the actual expense of turnover, it is the least costly.

With regard to integrity, every single member of security operations must be irreproachable. Security officers are all practicing human behaviorists, while working constantly with people. They must develop positive attitudes towards all divisions and departments. You must make certain that your staff has only the best interest of the company at heart and they are totally aware of their goals. Again, consider the development of your staff to perform closely related functions. Then consider doing functions that are not part of security, if they can be done without compromising your primary responsibility, or overtaxing your capabilities.

Traditionally, when selecting a security supervisor, an applicant required extensive law enforcement experience. Although such a background may be helpful for some protective functions today, it is not a prerequisite. Security operations today demand effective managers.

DIRECTION

Direction is managing or guiding subordinates on a daily basis, making sure they know the desired results in keeping with your organization's objectives, and insuring that the results are successfully achieved. While explaining the expected results, an effective manager shows his personnel how to complete tasks and also explains why they are required. While setting up guidelines for security officers, an opportune time presents itself for improving job skills. Effective communications is an extremely important quality for proper direction. Certain goals should be established within your department to insure proper direction of the security operations. Such goals should include, but not be limited to:

- Safeguard the assets of the firm
- Protect employees, visitors, and guests
- Be operations-oriented.
- Promote awareness for the necessity of security and safety
- Develop a program of protection services
- Assist in creating a pleasant environment.

- Be prepared for emergencies
- Market your security program through proper direction

Educational performance studies have recently revealed that a teacher's expectations of a student often affects his performance. The likelihood exists that if much is not expected, a student will not perform too well. Likewise, if good performance is expected, it is likely that the student will do well.

Don't expect miracles, however. Rather, good results should be the optimal goal. Be mindful of Murphy's Law: "Anything that can go wrong will!" Expect delays. Provide duties in rather general terms since potential problems cannot always be accurately predicted. Subordinates' perception of the importance of various tasks can often be assumed by the supervisor. However, like any other objective, its importance must be sold by the manager. While it may be admirable to pursue excellence, demanding perfection will stifle the planning of any change. Perfect solutions and excellence are great goals, but an effective manager can differentiate between idealism and practical techniques and consequences.

CONTROLLING

Controlling is overseeing your operations and regulating the actions of subordinates in an attempt to achieve the planned objectives. It is an exercise of authority determining and verifying the progress toward goals as established during the direction function. During this process, a manager collects information for comparison and takes any corrective action that may be required. The three elements of controlling are information gathering, comparison, and corrective action.

Methods of control include observing personnel, controlling the quality of the product/service, reviewing reports, monitoring statistics, utilizing budgets and audits. As previously discussed, a budget is both a plan and a mechanism of control that should be reviewed on a regular basis. Compensating adjustments may also have to be made if budgets are exceeded.

A controller is the financial watchdog in an organization. He oversees all financial activities and closely monitors production and sales activities. He must bring to the attention of the executive officers the overall investment and profit picture of the operation, and recommend possible changes or the implementation of specific activities.

Under the management function of *directing* in this chapter, we suggested some eight goals of the security department. A security supervisor must constantly review activity and incident reports to ensure that he is, in fact, exercising sufficient control over security operations. As one example, the first suggested goal was "safeguard the assets of the firm." That includes damage, waste, and theft, but let us concentrate on the last item for discussion.

Two necessary elements of theft are opportunity and inclination. Remove one of these factors and you prevent theft. Obviously, the first factor is the one subject to control. Someone's dishonest nature may never be altered. Therefore, adopt "Thou Shall Not Tempt" as your motto, and publicize it throughout your facility. You may wish to develop your own slogan, but try to make it catchy and not offensive. Using buttons, signs, and reminder decals and stickers promotes such an awareness campaign.

Now, to put theory into practice, exercise the three elements of control for each aspect of your established security department goals. Gather the necessary information (to identify thefts), compare the information (to establish patterns and narrow down a list of suspects), and take corrective action (remove the opportunity or provide necessary safeguards, such as alarms, locks, or CCTV, to prevent further losses or to apprehend thieves).

You should understand that sometimes excessive control costs will favor allowing some less costly mistakes or losses. Do not promote spending several thousand dollars to protect thirty dollars worth of scrap lumber.

In security management, proper control is a direct result of proper use of authority. A lack of control is a result of improper use of authority. An effective manager has to know himself and likewise know his staff—their abilities, personalities, and idiosyncracies. The golden rule, "Do unto others as you would have them do unto you," is an important tool of an effective manager. To retain control, be firm, but always fair!

ADDITIONAL POINTS

We have discussed the management functions of planning, organizing, staffing, directing, and controlling, and we will now just briefly review some other points for consideration.

An effective manager is an innovator. Innovation may include:

* Developing new ideas by the manager
* Continuing old ideas, with or without change, and combining them into new ideas
* Adapting ideas from other fields for your own use
* Promoting innovation by others
* Promoting cost effectiveness

A rather relaxed atmosphere is necessary to foster creative ideas. An organization must encourage this climate and also be willing to develop ideas with merit. One often hears comical stories concerning research and develpment divisions of major corporations who allow their Ph.D.s to work at will without set hours, without entry restrictions, and without other minor regulations such as dress codes, package passes, or parking. These tales relate some peculiar behavior by these "near-geniuses" that include nude walks into the woods to talk to nature, violin playing in the rain, and other seemingly strange activities.

Obviously, such relaxed regulations do compromise security. They can lead to costly experiences for the organization, including theft of expensive analytical equipment and industrial espionage. However, since most large and progressive concerns maintain and actively promote R & D, it obviously must be worth the expenditures and tolerance.

Remember, your position as a security manager, as with all other management positions, allows some room for innovation. Exercise innovation and encourage it from others.

Cooperation is the key to dealing with all other departments and activities within the organization. Be willing to assist others, formally and informally. Security is present to protect, prevent loss, and to assist. Close cooperation and understanding is mandatory from all areas in an organization to provide harmony. One word of caution in cooperative efforts, do not compromise your primary responsibilities.

However, cooperation, like communications, can be said to be a "subfunction" of the directing function. Effective communication is so important as a management activity that it appears as a separate chapter in this text.

SUMMARY

This chapter has addressed considerations for the security administrator or director. But, security supervisors must be aware of these responsibilities and functions if they aspire to promote themselves to a higher position of authority in a security operation.

Security is similar to every other operating department in your organization in that your executive officers want you first to be a manager, and then a security specialist. But do not be just another manager; be an effective manager!

MANAGEMENT FUNCTION CHECKLIST

YES NO
- ☐ ☐ 1. I continually update my files with new equipment, theories and methods.
- ☐ ☐ 2. I endeavor to forecast accurately and on a timely basis.
- ☐ ☐ 3. I define goals and establish realistic objectives to accomplish these goals.
- ☐ ☐ 4. I maintain a running log of activities.
- ☐ ☐ 5. I keep my superiors informed with monthly and yearly reports.

YES NO

☐   ☐   6.   I avoid procrastination.

☐   ☐   7.   I have initiated a formal planning process in my management techniques.

☐   ☐   8.   I prepare a budget realistically, with back-up justification for all costs.

☐   ☐   9.   I forecast the life expectancy of security equipment.

☐   ☐   10.   I am prepared to identify and justify how last year's allotment was spent.

☐   ☐   11.   I include current and projected staffing needs in my budget.

☐   ☐   12.   I distribute work loads evenly with clearly defined responsibilities.

☐   ☐   13.   I establish clear lines of communication.

☐   ☐   14.   I frequently analyze the department's philosophy, objectives and methods to see where improvements can be made.

☐   ☐   15.   I project a professional "manager" image.

☐   ☐   16.   Training is an integral part of my staffing function.

☐   ☐   17.   I demonstrate to my staff how to complete tasks and also explain why they are required.

☐   ☐   18.   I am operations oriented.

☐   ☐   19.   I collect information for comparison and take the necessary corrective action.

☐   ☐   20.   I always allow some room for innovation.

BIBLIOGRAPHY

Colling, Russell L.: *Hospital Security,* 1976, Security World Publishing Co., Inc. Los Angeles.

Dale, Ernest: *Management: Theory and Practice* (Second Edition), 1969. McGraw Hill Book Company, Chicago.

Drucker, Peter F.: *The Practice of Management,* 1954. Harper & Row Publishers, Inc. New York.

The Effective Executive, 1966. Harper & Row Publishers, Inc. New York.

Management: Tasks-Responsibilities-Practices, 1973. Harper & Row Publishers, Inc. New York.

Healy, Richard J. and Walsh, Timothy J.: *Industrial Security Management,* 1971. American Management Assoc. Inc. New York.

Hemphill, (Jr.) Charles F.: *Security for Business and Industry,* 1971. Dow Jones-Irwin, Inc., Homewood, Illinois.

Peter, Laurence J. and Hull, Raymond: *The Peter Principle,* 1969. Wm. Morrow & Co., Inc., New York.

Peter, Laurence J.: *The Peter Prescription,* 1972. Wm. Morrow & Co., Inc., New York.

4

Time Management

Often we hear people say, "There is just not enough time" to do everything they want to do or must do. In fact, most of us frequently mutter these exact words, if only to ourselves. Are you so busy that you cannot get anything done?

At quitting time, be it 8am, 3pm, 5pm, or 12 midnight, do you ever have all your work done? Did you accomplish everything you wanted to and everything everyone else wanted? The normal reply would be a disgusted "no." It is frustrating to have more work to do than time in which to do it. A successful man is one who has mastered his time and therefore his work.

You are familiar with the "high" you experience when you have completed a difficult report or project. It actually is an exhilarating occurrence. You would have never felt that sensation unless you planned and controlled the necessary time to achieve completion.

HOW TO IMPLEMENT TIME MANAGEMENT

You do not need to be an eccentric time nut, a super-efficiency expert, or a computerized time machine to master your time and make effective use of it.

The following suggestions are presented to make you a more competent security supervisor, and to assist you with your personal life. Some of the points may not have immediate value to you, but may serve to develop your competency upon your future growth in the business world. Thankfully, the day of the "night watchman" image of security has developed into the professionalism of a "security officer." However, you may wish to privately consider yourself to be a "time keeper," perhaps even a human, and highly valuable, pocket watch.

The following steps will be outlined to formulate how to manage your most valuable non-recoverable resource—time:

1. Analysis
2. Identification of problems
3. Control
4. Organization
   a. your time
   b. your work area
5. Avoiding procrastination

Analysis

The difference between time-consuming tasks and time-wasting tasks must be distinguished. Thereafter, any wasted time in the "consuming tasks" must be minimized. If you don't expend effort to achieve your goals or scheduled daily tasks, you are wasting time.

Conduct an analysis of your time. It need not be an exhaustive audit, but ascertain where the time goes. If you analyze your time on a daily or a weekly basis, you must assign some eight hours per day for sleep, several hours for grooming, travelling, schooling, reading, eating, entertainment (TV, movies, theater, music, hobbies, etc.), and possibly some "down time"—when you do absolutely nothing but relax or daydream.

After discounting these hours, you have your available working time. You might further differentiate between your "professional work" hours and your "personal work" hours. Now it is up to you to plan these periods accordingly to maximize the most effective use of your time.

Identification

Identify your time problems. Investigate their causes, and take the necessary corrective action to overcome time problems. Typical time wasters are:

- Procrastination—I'll get it done tomorrow

- Reading junk mail

- Telephone interruptions

- Sorting and re-sorting mail

- Lack of planning

- Lack of delegation

- Not being able to say "no"

- Failure to establish deadlines

- Condoning interruptions

- Overreacting to crisis situations

    Other time wasters might include: daydreaming, unnecessary reading material, unnecessary paperwork, shuffling that same paper, worry, tension, slow reading, guilt feelings, and striving for perfection. It would be extremely helpful to list your personal time wasters at the end of each workday, and identify how you or someone else wasted your time.

Control

When you achieve control of your time, you will then become a better decision-maker regarding the use of your time. To control your time, you must plan—and be conscious of it.

Planning is the most important function of management. It is always listed first under the description of a manager. As a security supervisor, you must identify yourself as a manager. You are getting work done through other people and you are directing many of their efforts. Planning, basically, is thinking in advance as a basis for doing things later.

For practical purposes, planning tells us where we are, where we have been, and where we are going. Reviewing plans permit us to check our progress, and retain our course or change it.

Your first step is to write down your long-range goals. What has to be done? When must it be done? Now do the same with your short-range goals. After completing the list, assign priorities. Do important tasks first. Get the things that count most done, or at least started, before you proceed to other tasks.

After setting priorities for your short-range and long-range goals, make a list of the things you can do this week to accomplish your listed goals. Rank and complete tasks in the value of their importance to you. Most importantly, you must take some action. Do them!

In your work, it is vital to have a daily list of things to be done. "To Do Lists" are commercially available, (see Figure 4-1), but you can design a similar list. Use 3 × 5 cards, 5 × 7 sheets, or anything else with which you feel comfortable. The important point is that you make a list every day at the same time, and, of course, that you follow it. The listing can be made for the next day just before you leave work or immediately upon your arrival. Cross off the items as you complete them, and make a new list, discarding yesterday's sheet every day after a review of your accomplishments. Carry uncompleted priority items to your new list. After preparing the list, assign priorities to the new list. Keep this list in front of you to serve as a constant reminder.

You have now started to initiate control of your time. Now you can concentrate on your priorities, since you have developed a system and are appropriately budgeting your time.

Include some flexibility in your daily schedule, because unforeseen events will interrupt you. Remember Murphy's Law, which basically states that if anything can go wrong, it will. But do not let interruptions frustrate you or

☞ Things to do today

_____ Date

1 _____ ☐

2 _____ ☐

3 _____ ☐

4 _____ ☐

5 _____ ☐

6 _____ ☐

7 _____ ☐

8 _____ ☐

9 _____ ☐

ABC COMPANY
Security & Safety Division

FIGURE 4-1.   Sample form. Things to do today.

prevent you from getting back to your work immediately. While it is valuable to consciously make all attempts to avoid interruptions, they will occur. Be attuned to positive distractions; they may in fact be opportunities.

Alternate your work with rest periods. Take a break for coffee, exercise, or even take a fifteen minute nap. Some consultant's have actually recommended installing a chinning bar in a manager's office. If you continue to work under constant pressure, you will diminish your effectiveness. Stop for a while and resume your work after being refreshed.

Sharpen your management abilities. Take the course that is being offered in your facility or at a nearby college or high school. When time permits, do some worthwhile reading. Everyone finds himself spending hours each week waiting—whether in a doctor's office, traffic, gas station, or someone's waiting room. Optimize that time by investing it in important reading.

Another important point should be considered, especially after successfully completing a difficult task. Leave some time and money to reward yourself. Treat yourself to a show, a fancy dinner, some new clothes, or even a vacation. And continue to be more aware of your time.

Organization of Your Time

In keeping with your major responsibilities, your identified goals as outlined on your daily schedule list, and your personal growth goals, decide what has to be done. Set your targets based on your organization's goals, your boss's goals, and your own goals. Know where you have been, where you are, where you are going, and how and when you will get there. Do not simulate the confusion of "The Mad Hatter." Plan your time and then allocate it. Decide what you want to do, schedule it, and then do it! Develop an organized system.

Identify your best time for thinking and working. If you get the most work done early in the morning, consider it your prime time and preserve it. Schedule your most difficult and demanding tasks during this prime time. Otherwise, schedule your activities around those uncontrollable events (e.g., meetings, conferences, appointments, etc.). Likewise, find your least productive periods and schedule minor tasks during them. Balance your time relatively between your most difficult problems and those of lesser importance.

Analyze your emotions and know how you react to people, projects, and problems. Knowing your strengths and limitations is extremely important. Do not imitate other supervisor's styles if you honestly feel that they do not suit you. Develop your own style and strive to continually professionalize it.

Screen your tasks and try to eliminate some and simplify others. Set a comfortable pace and do not try to do too much at once. Concentrate on one task at a time. Most importantly, do not fool yourself (or try to fool or impress others) by assuming that since you are extremely busy, you must be efficient. Remember, your goal is effectiveness—doing the right things right.

An effective manager, at any level, must learn to delegate. He simply cannot do everything himself. While it is sometimes ego-shattering, realize that you are not indispensable, and the building in which you work will most likely still be there after you leave.

A secretary is a vital key to effectiveness. However, if you are not blessed with this supportive staff member, look around at the people you are supervising. Assign tasks to your subordinates and develop their potential while increasing their value to you. Be sure, however, that you furnish sufficient information and guidance to allow them to complete the project successfully. The effective manager delegates responsibility to subordinates with only major matters referred to him for decision.

The concept of the "Quiet Hour" has been proposed by R. Alec Mackenzie in his book, *The Time Trap*.[11] Set up an hour a day to be alone, and isolate yourself to be able to concentrate. It can be from 9am to 10am to plan and organize your day, or it can be from 2pm to 3pm to allow time for reading, thinking, and planning. The secretary holds all calls except absolute emergencies and, if possible, will handle any requests for information. Furthermore, this person can list the calls and research any needed material, thereby cutting considerably the time required for your involvement. Calls can be transferred where applicable, to those who are capable of handling them. At the same time, she will act as an insulator to prevent unnecessary interruptions.

Control interruptions! Don't let the person get comfortable. Stand up and talk to him. Gently walk the person out of your office or schedule a quick meeting of the topic at some more convenient time (for you) unless it is an actual emergency. There are many techniques that can be developed to keep unwanted or unnecessary trespassing by others to a minimum. Consider closing your door and locking it! With lengthy telephone callers (over three minutes), lie a little to get them off the line and away from your time.

Learn how to say "no." Don't be a hero or a savior to others at the expense of your time. Don't volunteer your efforts if the commitment will detract from or destroy your schedule or pending projects.

Improve your managerial skills, especially communications. Learn also how to listen to others. It will assist you in following directions and understanding the needs of others. Improve your reading capabilities. Be selective in your choice of material. Read books and newspapers and skim over irrelevant sections.

Also strive to improve your writing techniques. Write short letters, memoranda, and reports. Write to express, not to impress; and keep it clear, concise, and complete. Reduce your paperwork by drafting a reply on an inquiry, and let the secretary compose the letter. Also try to write a response on the bottom of a request. Only make a photostatic copy if it is necessary.

Have shorter and more productive meetings. Review the times, frequency, and duration of these "time wasters." Perhaps they can be held during your lower-productivity periods in the late afternoons. Perhaps instead of weekly sessions, they could be held but twice, or once a month. Meetings have a tendency to become congenial and informal gatherings, and they last entirely too long. The chairperson should be encouraged to have a written

[11]For further reading, see MacKenzie, R. Alec, *The Time Trap*, McGraw-Hill, New York, 1972.

agenda and then forced to stick to it. Perhaps meetings could be shortened by being held in your office, over coffee, or during lunch. Meetings might even be eliminated by discussions over the telephone.

Encourage others to manage their own time and to respect yours.

Organization of Your Work Area

Avoid the crowded desk syndrome. Use your desk as a work center, not as an open file cabinet. This applies to you as a security supervisor whether you have a desk of your own, or use a table in a "squad room" setting or a communications center. Use file folders for organization, and ensure that you have sufficient supplies and equipment to perform all of your functions.

Remember that neatness gives an allusion of being well organized. Even if you are not attempting to impress others that you are busy by maintaining a disorderly desk, you will look disorganized, and possibly lazy. The chances also are good that you are not delegating work properly.

Keep unneeded things out of reach and, if possible, out of sight. Distractions, again, must be minimized. Look at your office and the location of the desk. Perhaps you can rearrange the position of your desk to prevent others from catching your attention while walking by, and likewise combat your own habit of watching everything that is going on outside of your office. Close your door and do not perpetuate the old and discarded supervisor's "Open Door" policy to allow subordinates to come in whenever they want to do so. If necessary, consider moving your office to an isolated area.

Avoiding Procrastination

Procrastination leads to mental and physical fatigue. It is rarely, if ever, worth the pain or the pressure. Do things when your energy effectiveness, and time are optimal.

If you hesitate extensively with difficult or unpleasant tasks, you must analyze your motives and find the cause of your inaction. All habits can be changed. If you are afraid to make a mistake by doing something wrong, forget it. Usually the consequences are not tragic, so do them and get them out of your way. If you find certain projects unpleasant, think of how much more unpleasant they become by not doing them. Also, do not even think about doing things that do not have to be done. Again, be selective and, thereby, effective.

The quality of your work will suffer if you wait until the last minute. Other people may not cooperate with your immediate deadline. They may not be available for consultation or able to furnish you with your needed data. Unanticipated interruptions, other time wasters, or another crisis may further delay your project.

Do the hard jobs first and get them out of your way. Once under control, these tasks prove not as bad as you had expected. Always limit your time on trivial matters.

If something is worth doing, do it—or forget it.

WHEN AND WHERE TO USE TIME MANAGEMENT

The emphasis in this chapter has been on managing time in your professional life. Your personal life, however, should also be effectively controlled with regard to your most valuable resource. Your personal goals should be likewise identified, analyzed, and evaluated. Thereafter, a time schedule should be made to maintain your course appropriately. A college student would certainly be foolish not to carefully schedule his classes and leave all the difficult and required courses to be taken during the last few semesters.

We all set personal goals for ourselves, if only once a year as New Year's resolutions. Perhaps you want to lose some weight, resume your exercise program, stop smoking, read more often, return to, or complete your schooling. Make a time schedule of both long- and short-range goals for yourself. Then monitor it to ensure your progress. Drop that 15 pounds, join the ''Y,'' give up all tobacco, earn that degree.

Your habits and routines should be examined. Are you spending too much time viewing ridiculous television programs? What are you reading? What about your other activities? If you find them nonrewarding, cut them out and apply your time in more stimulating areas.

As an interested officer in the security department, you might focus on these goals:

- If you are a Sergeant   —   become a Lieutenant, Captain
- If you are a Supervisor —   become the Director of Security
                                (in your organization or in
                                another firm)
- If you are the Director —   break into upper management

Getting promoted is not a passive act only remotely involving you. One graduates from college after much time and some difficulty, pretty much by personal initiative. You, therefore, promote yourself through your ability, basic, intelligence, honesty, and obvious interest in advancement.

Returning to your professional goals, get the secretary to assist you with the paperwork and have him do the menial tasks. If a secretary is not possible due to budgetary restraints, then delegate some of that work to a subordinate. Consider the completion or revision of these pending projects:

- Audit of your Alarm/CCTV Systems

- Lost & Found Valuables Procedure

- Increase Training for your Security Staff

- Update Property Passes

- Revise Visitor Control Procedures

- Introduce an Identification Card System

- Parking and Traffic Control

- Shipping and Receiving Procedures

- Reorganization of the Security Operations

FIFTY TIME-SAVING IDEAS[12]

Telephone

1. Use "call forwarding" feature during your "no interruptions" period.
2. Have calls screened.
3. Schedule a time at which you will be available to receive calls each day.
4. Use phone rather than visit person involved.
5. Leave message rather than calling again.
6. Jot down points you want to make before telephoning.
7. Keep calls brief and businesslike.
8. Catch early birds before start of day. Catch late birds at end of day.
9. Leave a message when not too complex.
10. Speak to someone else when called party is unavailable.

Written

1. Send time limit response memos.
2. Send action-if-no-response memos.
3. After sorting, handle each piece of paper only once.
4. Use margin replies instead of memos.
5. Jot down notes before dictating.
6. When you read a letter, jot down outline of reply.
7. Abbrev. wherever poss.

    [12]McGuigan, Jack, "One Hundred Time Saving Ideas," *Cooperative Education Quarterly*, Volume 2 1, May/July, 1979, pp. 13-15.

8. Don't read incoming mail unless you plan to begin action on each piece requiring action.
9. Make notes so as not to burden your memory.
10. File notes where they are likely to be found.

Meetings

1. Schedule as many appointments as possible during the same part of the week.
2. Hold informal meetings standing up.
3. Hold formal meetings just before lunch or late in the afternoon.
4. Set start and end times for all meetings and stick to them.
5. Start meetings on time even if someone is missing.
6. Send premeeting agenda and notes. Ask participants to come prepared for decisions and actions.
7. Clarify and stick to the purpose of the meeting.
8. Meet in some place other than your office so you can leave.
9. Offer to discuss the question over lunch.
10. Hold meetings in a conference room or a place where you won't be interrupted.

Interruptions

1. Anticipate, avoid and manage interruptions.
2. Isolate yourself when you need uninterrupted time.
3. Start day early and leave early to avoid interruptions.
4. Ask the purpose of the visit.
5. Remain standing. Don't offer visitor a seat.
6. If visitor needs more than five minutes, schedule a meeting.
7. Tell visitor you have a meeting coming up.
8. Minimize the duration of interruptions.
9. Group interruptions (informal meetings?)
10. Keep an annoying poster on the wall.

Managerial

1. Delegate whenever possible.
2. Require completed work from subordinates and team members.
3. Develop subordinates so they can take on more complex tasks.
4. Set deadlines and checkpoints for control of delegated tasks.
5. Encourage others to depend on themselves rather than on you.

6.   Rely on others to do their job. Don't second guess them.
7.   Have certain mail routed directly to subordinates.
8.   Quit doing other supervisors' work.
9.   Make list: to do, to see, to call, to write.
10. Set deadlines and checkpoints.

TIME MANAGEMENT CHECKLIST

YES NO

☐ ☐ 1.   I realize that time is my most valuable resource.
☐ ☐ 2.   I have analyzed my time and have identified my time problems.
☐ ☐ 3.   I have decided to allocate my time effectively.
☐ ☐ 4.   I have prepared an activity list both for long- and short-range goals.
☐ ☐ 5.   I have initiated my daily activity list.
☐ ☐ 6.   I have identified the priorities.
☐ ☐ 7.   I have decided to do my priority projects first.
☐ ☐ 8.   I recognize the need for order in my professional career and personal life.
☐ ☐ 9.   I have reduced "pushing paper" and handle each piece only once.
☐ ☐ 10. I have learned that delegation saves my time and develops my subordinates.
☐ ☐ 11. I will tie my own goals with those of the organization and my immediate supervisor.
☐ ☐ 12. I have identified my "prime time" and my least productive periods.
☐ ☐ 13. I have analyzed my emotions.
☐ ☐ 14. I will develop my own style.
☐ ☐ 15. I concentrate on only one task at a time.
☐ ☐ 16. I control interruptions.
☐ ☐ 17. I have learned to say "no."
☐ ☐ 18. I will have shorter meetings.
☐ ☐ 19. I encourage others to manage their time and respect mine.
☐ ☐ 20. I have organized my desk and office.
☐ ☐ 21. I screen and separate all incoming correspondence and requests.
☐ ☐ 22. If I cannot complete a project, I take some action on it.
☐ ☐ 23. I keep my daily activity list in front of me.
☐ ☐ 24. I will invest my time.
☐ ☐ 25. I minimize any wasted time.

YES NO
☐ ☐ 26. I realize that controlling my time will make me a better decision maker regarding my time usage.
☐ ☐ 27. I recognize planning as one of the most important functions of management.
☐ ☐ 28. I have included flexibility in my schedule for unforeseen events.
☐ ☐ 29. I make use of my waiting time for important reading.
☐ ☐ 30. I will sharpen my management abilities, especially Communications.
☐ ☐ 31. I will improve my reading and writing techniques.
☐ ☐ 32. I will reward myself.
☐ ☐ 33. I will limit junk mail, useless magazines, etc.
☐ ☐ 34. I have removed distractions.
☐ ☐ 35. I realize that procrastination is not worth the pain or the pressure.
☐ ☐ 36. I will start to enjoy my time.

BIBLIOGRAPHY

Bliss, Edwin C.: *Getting Things Done: The ABC's of Time Management.* New York: Charles Scribner's Sons, 1976.

Drucker, Peter F.: *The Effective Executive.* New York: Harper & Row, 1966.

Drucker, Peter F.: *MANAGEMENT: Tasks, Responsibilities, Practices.* New York:

Franklin, Benjamin: *Sayings of Poor Richard.* Westwood, N.J.: Fleming H. Revell Co., 1960 (From *Poor Richard's Almanac).* Philadelphia: B. Franklin, Printer, 1732.

Goudsmit, Samuel A., Claiborne, Robert and the Editors of *Life: Time.* New York: Time Incorporated, 1966.

Harris, Thomas A. (MD): *I'm OK - You're OK.* New York: Harper & Row, 1969.

Lakein, Alan: *How to Get Control of Your Time and Your Life.* New York: Peter H. Wyden Publishers, 1973.

Mackenzie, R. Alec: *The Time Trap,* New York: McGraw-Hill Book Company, 1972.

McCay, James T.: *The Management of Time.* Englewood Cliffs, N.J.: Prentice-Hall, Inc., 1959.

McGuigan, Jack: "One Hundred Time Saving Ideas," *Cooperative Education Quarterly,* Vest Inc., May/July, Vol. 2, No. 1, 1979. pp.12-15.

Novack, Bernard: "Managing Time," *Cooperative Education Quarterly,* Vest Inc. August/October 1979, Vol. 2, No. 2, pp.16-22.

Peter, Dr. Laurence J. and Hull, Raymond: *The Peter Principle.* New York: William Morrow & Co., Inc., 1969.

Sayles, Leonard R. and Strauss, George: *Human Behavior in Organizations.* Englewood Cliffs, N.J.: Prentice-Hall, Inc., 1966.

Toffler, Alvin, *Future Shock.* New York: Random House, 1970.

Whyte, William H., Jr.: *The Organizational Man.* New York: Simon and Schuster, 1956.

5
Effective Communications

The successful leadership role of a supervisory officer often depends on the officer's ability to communicate. Very few people will argue with the statement that "communication is the key to effective leadership." No leader can be effective or maintain good relations with security officers, and the general public, unless he can communicate.

Communication is an act of transmitting information (orders, reports) to a receiver. Effective communication does not take place unless the receiver, an individual or a group, understands the information being transmitted.

Effective communication, therefore, is concerned with the interaction of people; the transmitting information; the conveying of concepts and ideas; the understanding of what is being transmitted; the timeliness of relaying information; and the responsiveness to the transmitted information. Each of these elements is essential to effective communication and leadership.

INTERACTION

Effective interaction and effective communication go hand-in-hand. The absence of interaction between individuals, between an individual and a group, or between groups is often an indicator of poor communications. Interaction requires communication, whether it be oral, written, or body language. Not all interaction is positive. Two people fighting are interacting. In this case it is negative interaction. Positive and frequent interaction, on the other hand, allows effective communication to take place in a downward, upward, and horizontal flow. People must interact and share information, if effective communication is to take place in the organization.

Further, communication in the interaction process is not simply telling someone to do something. Positive interaction and understanding of the communication process must take place when the supervisory officer relays information from management to subordinates. How the information is relayed by the supervisor will determine how well the information, whether it be a policy procedure or clarification of a memorandum, will be adopted by subordinates.

DOWNWARD COMMUNICATION

Downward communication is the flow of information downward through the chain of command. In security, the downward flow usually occurs in the form of orders. Security officers are given instructions, often dealing with security policy or procedures, to implement in the field. These instructions must not be vague or incomplete. Since the security supervisor is responsible for transmitting information to subordinates, it is essential that he understands and practices the following rules for effective communication.

- The information must always be accurate and complete. The effective leader will plan what to say to subordinates. The information should be presented in a logical, sequential order. Avoid unnecessary information, since it might confuse the listener. It is vital, however, to present all the facts in a clear and accurate manner.
- The information must be timely. Information that arrives too late for action is useless. In the case of security emergency operations, information that arrives too late can be disastrous.
- Your language has to be understood. If you use words or slang that the listener does not understand, there is a good possibility that your message will be misunderstood.
- Always afford the listener the opportunity to ask questions. You should encourage your subordinates to ask questions whenever they are in doubt. The ideal time to clarify a point, whether it be a policy, an order, or a procedure, is when you are presenting the new information to your subordinates. Confusion, as well as inaccurate results, can occur if your subordinates misunderstand the information.
- Have your subordinates summarize, in their own words, the information you presented to them. The instant feedback will indicate whether your subordinates understand the basic facts of who, what, when, where, why and how.

A major portion of the downward communication process is in order transmittal. The supervisory officer is responsible for issuing orders, as well as to seeing that the orders are properly implemented. It is imperative that supervisory officers issue orders in a clear, complete and professional manner that is easily acceptable by the subordinate. The order should contain all the information to the questions of who, what, when, where, why, and how. The order should also be issued in an ethical and fair manner. It is wise to place yourself in the other person's shoes by asking yourself the question: "Is this the way I would want someone to issue an order to me?" Remember, the tone of voice can mean the difference between acceptance and rejection by the subordinate.

Finally, clarify the reasons behind the order. Explaining the "why" for issuing an order will often help eliminate any personal feelings about it.

UPWARD COMMUNICATION

Upward communication in the security field is usually concerned with reports.

Administration is interested in a permanent record of information. Reports provide the administration with past and current events, while serving as a basis for future administrative decisions.

Statistical reports, forwarded upward, provide pertinent information to administration on incident occurrences, such as safety hazards, fire hazards, thefts, parking violations, property damage, or unauthorized intruders. Other reports include information on man-hours consumed, the deployment of the security force, personnel discharged for security violations, operational procedures, budget requests, exceptional events, and anticipated problems. Communication flowing upward should also include suggestions, ideas and plans, grievances, complaints, and rumors. Figures 5-1 and 5-2 are sample reports of upward communication.

Information flowing upward does not always reach the top-level administrator because of what is commonly known as "people filters." All along the chain of command, both in an upward and downward flow, information is filtered as it passes through each level. Filters occur when individuals believe that certain information should be added or deleted. The filtering process in the upward flow is more severe than in the downward flow.

Some common filters applied to upward communications, as listed in the *Army Military Leadership Manual*, 7M22-100, are:

- The notion that any opinion in opposition to a superior's idea is "negative thinking" and therefore bad.
- The notion that employees always gripe, and you should only worry when they don't.
- The belief that the information is unimportant and that the originator does not have the big picture in mind.
- The belief that you will get into trouble for passing along this type of information.
- The belief that superiors are not interested in the information.
- The belief that the information will reflect adversely on you, your ability, or your shift.
- The belief that your superiors only want to be told the good things and not the bad things.

Not all filters are bad. Many serve a useful purpose. It is up to the first-line supervisor to determine what is significant information that should be passed up the line. The acid test is to ask yourself whether you would need or like to have this information if you were the next leader up in the organization. If the answer is yes, pass it up the chain of command.

COMMUNICATION ON A HORIZONTAL LEVEL

Not all communication takes place in an upward or downward direction. Much communication takes place horizontally, where security supervisors interact

---

MONTHLY INCIDENT OCCURRENCE REPORT

| _____ | _____ | _____ |
| (Month) | (Year) | (Location) |

Instructions: This report is to be compiled by the security supervisor within five working days of the month, following the reporting month, and forwarded to the corporate office.

Type of Incident   *Number of Occurrences*

Assault   _____
Petty Theft   _____
Grand Larceny   _____
Fire   _____
Property Damage   _____
Vandalism   _____
Auto Accidents   _____
Personal Injury   _____
List others:

_____   _____
_____   _____
_____   _____

Supervisor's narrative report:

_____   _____
Signature of security supervisor   (date)
completing this report

FIGURE 5-1.   Sample report of upward communication. Summary of daily activities.

with other security supervisors. The type of communication exchanged at this level is informative. Problems are discussed, suggestions and alternatives are given, issues are raised, and formal, as well as informal, training takes place.

The flow of information on the horizontal level is not as restricted as upward or downward communication. Information on the horizontal level is informal, whereas information upward or downward is usually formal. Information usually exchanged at this level does not concentrate on giving orders. Rather, horizontal communication focuses on providing helpful suggestions to mutual problems. At least, this is the ideal manner in which communication should take place. Beware, however, because a great deal of misinformation can be exchanged.

SUMMARY OF DAILY ACTIVITIES
SECURITY DEPARTMENT

TO: DIRECTOR, SECURITY   DATE: _____

From: _____   DATE COVERED: _____

Hours worked   Capt: _____ LT: _____ SGT: _____ GUARD: _____ TOTAL: _____

Break in hours _____ Men late _____ Men absent _____ Daily 286's Submitted _____

Calls answered 111 ____ 333 ____ 444 ____ 555 ____ 666 ____ Other ____ TOTAL _____

Parking violations _____ Summons issued _____

Doors found open, list locations: _____ TOTAL _____

Visitor passes collected _____ Visitor pass numbers from _____ To _____

Property passes collected _____ Packages checked _____

Vehicles entering shipping & receiving _____ TOTAL PERSONS CHECKED _____

Key stations checked 4-12 Shift _____ 12-8 Shift _____ TOTAL _____

Door alarms checked _____ Alarms not working _____

Equipment broken _____ Equipment missing _____

Safety hazards_____

Suspicious persons observed _____ Suspicious vehicles observed _____

Indicents reported _____ Incidents investigated _____ Floor _____

Department _____ Room number _____ Type incident _____

Accidents reported motor vehicle _____ Personal injury _____ TOTAL _____

Trips to court _____ Other trips outside company premises _____ TOTAL TRIPS _____

Reports turned in _____ Fire drills _____

Special details: _____
_____

Remarks: _____
_____
_____
_____

FIGURE 5-2.   Sample report of upward communication. Monthly incident occurrence report.

The Grapevine

It is at the horizontal level that the ''grapevine'' or ''rumor mill'' flourishes. Information at this level moves freely, often at a much faster pace than the upward or downward flow through the chain of command. Because of this, the grapevine is used extensively in all organizations.

The grapevine should not be viewed as harmful. It often helps you to identify problems within your area. It also helps you determine how new policies are being accepted in the field.

The grapevine system usually contains incomplete information or information which does not make sense. No one likes to transmit or accept information which does not make sense or is incomplete. So grapevine information is usually ''massaged'' to make good sense. Additional information is invented and added to partial information as it passes through the grapevine system. It is extremely important for the supervisory officer to provide sufficient information to his subordinates to reasonably explain whatever situation is at hand.

It is also important for the individual who receives grapevine information to weigh known facts, seek official clarification and transmit correct, as well as total, information to his staff.

EFFECTIVE LISTENING

Hearing is not the same as listening. You can hear a radio playing, a phonograph record playing or a person speaking, and still not be listening to what is actually occurring.

Webster's Seventh New Collegiate Dictionary defines "hearing" as "the process, function, or power of perceiving sound." The same dictionary defines "listen" as "to pay attention to sound" and "to hear with thoughtful attention." The difference, then, between hearing and listening is *attention*. The listener must concentrate on what the speaker is saying.

Studies have shown that most people listen at only 25 per cent efficiency. It is not surprising if you consider that the average person speaks at a rate of 125 to 150 words a minute. The human mind is capable of conscious thought at a rate that is four or five times faster than that. Only one-fourth of the human mind is occupied with listening to the speaker's words.

With only a fourth of our mind occupied by a speaker, 75 per cent of the listener's mind is free to think of counter-arguments, to daydream, to rush ahead and try to anticipate the speaker's conclusion, or to dwell on a specific point that the speaker made. The problem with any of these situations is that we may linger too long on our sidetrack and miss the important points the speaker was trying to convey.

Still another problem exists in the listening process. People have a tendency to forget 50 per cent of what they heard the previous day. This is further compounded by the fact that as time elapses, the listener may forget as much as 75 per cent of what they are supposed to know when it's time to use the information.

There is, however, a way to improve our listening comprehension. It doesn't happen overnight. It requires careful attention to a few basic rules. If followed, they will increase the listener's comprehension and they will assist the supervisor in becoming a more effective leader.

Basic Rules to Improve Listening Skills

1. *Be attentive.* You have to be determined to keep your mind on what the speaker is saying. You may still become momentarily distracted by outside elements, such as someone entering the room. You should not,

however, allow yourself to be taken up by the distraction. You have to refocus your attention back to the speaker.

2. *Listen to the message, and not the delivery.* Too often, many listeners get caught in the trap of concentrating on the speaker's poor delivery instead of concentrating on the content of the delivery. It is the message that counts, not the appearance or mannerisms of the speaker.

3. *Avoid concentrating on emotionally-charged words.* Certain words have a tendency to arouse the emotions of the listener. Words such as "pig," "communist," "male chauvinist," "crook," "mother-in-law," and "coward," are emotionally upsetting words for a good number of individuals. The listener has to learn to control his emotions and not let the individual charged words distract you from understanding the message of speaker.

4. *Strive for accurate perception.* It is important that the listener and the speaker have the same understanding of what was said. Meanings, and interpretations of what was said, can be different for the speaker and the listener. A good practice is to repeat back to the speaker what was said. This is especially true when issuing orders. By having the subordinate repeat back to the supervisor the orders issued, both agree what is to be done.

5. *Go after ideas, not memorized facts.* It is a fallacy to think the average individual can memorize all the facts that a speaker presents. The effective listener concentrates on focusing on central ideas, not a series of memorized facts. Trying to memorize a series of facts will only distract you, causing you to concentrate on memorizing the speaker's initial facts. While memorizing the initial facts, you half hear the following facts, and may entirely miss the essential facts. The effective listener, then listens attentively to ideas. Once the central idea is understood, the supporting facts seem to fall into place in your mind.

6. *Screen and weigh what is being said.* An important part of listening is analyzing what is being heard. You have to discount those points that are not relevant to the speaker's topic and concentrate on those points that have bearing on it. Weigh the speakers' evidence against what you know to be a fact. Important questions to ask yourself are: "How valid is the evidence?" and "How complete is the evidence?"

BARRIERS TO EFFECTIVE COMMUNICATION

Effective communication does not just happen. It has to be cultivated and maintained by each and every security officer. In order to reduce the possibility of communication breakdown, the security officer should avoid the following communication barriers:

- Distortion—Messages that are transmitted unclearly become distorted as they progress up or down the chain of command. When the message is complex or confusing, the security supervisor must make it clear that if subordinates do not understand messages they should question them.

- **Don't talk *at* people, talk *to* them**—No one wants to be spoken to in a manner that is degrading. Voice, tone, volume, emphasis and body expression are important aspects of communication. One does not lose leadership authority by talking to people.
- **Lack of trust**—How you handle information reported to you will determine what will be reported to you in the future. If subordinates feel that you have betrayed their confidence or that you have failed to act on items they report, they simply will not trust you with information in the future.
- **Personality clashes and power struggles**— If two sergeants are openly trying to outdo each other to get the Lieutenant's job, the communication within security will become strained or non-existent. Communication at the horizontal level will deteriorate as each tries to outdo the other in order to make themselves look good at the expense of the other. If the struggle lasts long enough, it will permeate throughout the system, with subordinates taking sides and thus further reducing the communication process.

NONVERBAL COMMUNICATION

The spoken word is not the only way in which to communicate with others. Body movements can say as much, if not more, than words. We may be saying one thing while our bodies are conveying an entirely different story. For example - the security supervisor sitting at his desk writing a memo, saying to a subordinate, who wants to discuss a suggestion for improving a particular security operation, that he's "all ears." The subordinate begins to tell his suggestion to the supervisor, but the supervisor continues to write while the subordinate speaks. The security supervisor's words "I'm all ears" imply that he is interested in what the subordinate has to say. The supervisor's actions, however, say loud and clear that he is not genuinely interested in the subordinate's suggestion. At least, this is what the supervisor's actions convey to the subordinate.

It may be that the supervisor can listen and write at the same time. The subordinate, however, has something to say and expects the superior's undivided attention. If the supervisor cannot stop what he is doing because it is an emergency rush assignment, he should have told the subordinate that he cannot see him then. He should explain that his rush assignment would prohibit him from paying full attention to the proposed suggestion. The supervisor should then ask the subordinate to see him later, giving the subordinate a precise time (appointment) for the subsequent meeting.

The above situation is but one example that points out how our actions and/or body movements convey messages. What we are discussing is "Body Languages." It is hand movements, facial expressions, and body positioning.

It takes into consideration how we sit, how we stand and how we look at someone when we speak.

Body language is always present when communicating verbally in the
presence of another individual. We use physical gestures and facial expressions
to emphasize a point, to change the meaning of a word, to express our attitudes and our feelings (see Figure 5-3). When used correctly, this enhances our
effective communication.

Nonverbal communication	Some interpretations
Silence	Contempt
	Anger
	Sorrow
	Boredom
	Meditation
	Snobbishness
	Fear
	Shyness
	Concentration
Tears	Joy
	Sorrow
	Love
	Pain
A wink	Hi—how are you?
	Don't give away the secret
	Come on over to my table
	A signal
	Disregard—pay no attention
Shake a fist	Defy
	Threaten
	Power
	Warning
Cross one's fingers	Make a wish
	Good luck sign
	It wipes out the lie
	Hope
Arms folded at chest	Stand-offish
	Mean
	Hard
	Worried
	Upset
	Urgent

FIGURE 5.3.   Nonverbal communications and their interpretations.

Nonverbal communication	Some interpretations
Hand shake	Hello
	Goodby
	How are you?
	I'm sorry
	Peace
	Sportsmanship
Smile	Warm
	Greeting
	Humor
	Happiness
	Flirtation
	Good-natured
	Ridicule
	Snicker
	Grin
	Affection

Figure 5-3 continued.

COMMUNICATION CHECKLIST

YES NO

☐ ☐ 1. I listen attentively to others without interrupting.

☐ ☐ 2. I do not do all of the talking.

☐ ☐ 3. I take measures to insure that the person I am communicating with understands my message.

☐ ☐ 4. I look at the person, eye to eye, when I am speaking.

☐ ☐ 5. I stay alert and try to grasp what other people are saying.

☐ ☐ 6. I convey all the facts in a clear, accurate and impartial manner.

☐ ☐ 7. I use words and phrases that have common meanings for the person to whom I am speaking.

☐ ☐ 8. I endeavor to generate positive interaction with people.

☐ ☐ 9. I encourage the listener to ask questions for greater clarity.

☐ ☐ 10. My body language conveys sincere interest in what the other person is saying.

☐ ☐ 11. I am ethical and fair in my communication with everyone with whom I work.

☐ ☐ 12. I listen for meanings and ideas and not just words.

☐ ☐ 13. I speak and write to convey meaning in a manner easily understood.

YES NO

☐ ☐ 14. I prepare reports for completeness and brevity, answering the six critical questions of who, what, when, where, why and how.

☐ ☐ 15. I submit information and reports on time.

☐ ☐ 16. I share pertinent information with all those who have a need to know in all matters affecting the performance of their jobs.

☐ ☐ 17. I do not divulge classified information to unauthorized individuals.

☐ ☐ 18. I give clear and complete orders in a professional manner that is easy to accept by the subordinate.

☐ ☐ 19. I am careful in relaying instructions so that they can be carried out in the manner in which they were intended.

☐ ☐ 20. I assume the blame when my attempts to communicate are unsuccessful.

BIBLIOGRAPHY

Bureau of Business Practices: *Communications, Portfolios One through Twelve.* 1965.

Headquarters, Department of the Army: *Military Leadership* (7M 22-100), Washington, D.C. Chapter 11, June 1963.

Nichols, Ralph G.: *Listening is a 10-part skill, Managing Yourself,* Nation's Business, Washington, D.C.

Redfield, Charles E.: *Communications in Management,* University of Chicago Press, Chicago, Ill. 1963.

The International Association of Chiefs of Police Professional Standards Division: *Police Reference Notebook, Supervision, Section Eleven,* Chapter 11E, Garthersburg, Md, 1974.

The United States Jaycees: *Leadership in Action Workbook,* Co-sponsored by Massachusetts Mutual Life Insurance Company (25M 171), Chapter II, October, 1970.

Wanat, John A, Brown, John F. and Connin, Lawrence C.: *Hospital Security Guard Training Manual.* Springfield, Thomas Chapter 17, 1977.

Xerox Corporation: *Effective Listening—Listener's Response Book,* New York, N.Y. 1967.

6

Delegation, Authority and Control[13]

An essential role of the supervisor is to delegate work so that company operations can run smoothly, efficiently and profitably. When a supervisor delegates an assignment, he must also delegate the authority and responsibility to carry out the assignment.

"Let others take care of the details." That, in a few words, is the meaning of delegating work and responsibility.

In theory, the same principles for getting work done through other people apply whether you have 25 employees and one top assistant or 150 to 200 employees and several key people. Yet, putting the principles into practice is often difficult.

Delegation is perhaps the hardest job security supervisors have to learn. Some never do. Some insist on handling many details and work themselves into early graves. Others pay lip service to the idea but actually run a one-man operation. They give their subordinates many responsibilities but little or no authority.

TIPS ON DELEGATING EFFECTIVELY

- Know your subordinates' capabilities
- Assign tasks that are challenging and within your subordinates' ability to accomplish
- Clearly identify what is to be done, paying particular attention to who is to do what and when
- Allow subordinates to perform in their own style
- Designate sufficient authority and control to get the work done
- Hold subordinates responsible for their actions
- Maintain a positive check, feedback, on your subordinates' progress

HOW MUCH AUTHORITY?

Questions that supervisors must constantly ask themselves are:

[13]Portions of this chapter were adopted from *Delegating Work and Responsibility*, Small Business Administration, Management Aids No. 191, September, 1967.

1. How much authority and control do I have?
2. How much authority and control should I delegate?

The answer to both of the above questions must always be "sufficient authority to get the job done."

The supervisor's function should be spelled out in a written job description. The description should include the supervisor's duties, responsibilities and authority. By the same token, the supervisor should provide his subordinates with a job description that delineates their duties, responsibilities and authority.

It is also essential for the supervisor to work out practices and procedures with his subordinates. This type of information is necessary to get the job done. By establishing written practices and procedures, it is a lot easier to identify overlaps or gaps in assigned responsibilities. It also identifies to all concerned parties that for which they are being held responsible. By developing a procedural manual, each supervisor and each subordinate has a detailed statement of the function of the security department and the extent of their authority. The following basic duties and responsibilities are typical of security operations in each rank. This type of description can be used in a written job description and/or in a security procedural manual.

1. *Captain.* A security captain is the highest ranking officer assigned to an assistant or chief security director. The captain generally serves as the officer in charge of one of the tours of duty, with direct supervision of the security lieutenant(s) and security sergeant(s) and overall supervision of the security officers (guards) on his relief. He carries out the orders and instructions of the security director or assistant director. In the absence of the chief security director and/or his assistant, he acts for the director. He assigns security officers to their tour, makes daily inspections, trains lieutenants to act in his place during his absence, advises the director of unusual happenings, acts as a rating officer for subordinates, and remains within his area of responsibility until properly relieved, advising headquarters of his whereabouts at all times while on duty.

2. *Lieutenant.* When a lieutenant is the highest ranking officer, his duties and responsibilities are the same as those of a captain. When under the supervision of a captain, the lieutenant generally serves as the officer in charge of one of the tours of duty, with direct supervision of security sergeants and overall supervision of the security officers on his relief. He carries out the orders and instructions of the captain and, in his absence, acts for the captain. He assigns security officers on his relief, makes daily inspections, trains sergeants to act in his place during his absence, advises the captain of unusual happenings, acts as a rating officer for subordinates, and remains within his area of responsibility until properly relieved, advising headquarters of his whereabouts at all times while on duty.

3. *Sergeant.* When the sergeant is the highest ranking officer, his duties and responsibilities are the same as a captain or lieutenant, as the situation

indicates. When under the supervision of a lieutenant, he exercises direct supervision over security officers (guards) within his area. He carries out the orders and instructions of the lieutenant, and in his absence, assumes his authority and responsibilities. He makes patrol and building inspections, advises his superior of security activities and unusual events, trains security officers to act for him in his absence, evaluates the performance of security officers under his jurisdiction, and maintains contact with headquarters, remaining within his area of responsibility until properly relieved.

4. *Security officer.* A security officer (guard) is under the immediate supervision of a sergeant. His job is to protect the building(s) and grounds to which he is assigned, including the contents, occupants, and visitors and to make patrols as assigned. He seeks out and takes immediate protective action against existing hazards or conditions which may cause damage, injury, or interference through fire, accident, theft, or trespass, and reports such conditions or hazards by using established security forms. He enforces security regulations where applicable, handles lost and found articles, enforces rules and regulations governing the building and directs traffic. He uses special police authority when it is vested in him to make arrests for cause or, when no such authority exists, calls upon available law enforcement personnel to make necessary arrests. He maintains order on his post and helps persons requiring assistance or information, observes good security practices and standards, and performs such other duties as are assigned.[14]

If a supervisor is to run a successful security operation, he must delegate authority properly. How much authority is proper will depend on a given situation. Always remember that authority is the fuel that makes the machine go when you delegate work and responsibility. Don't let pride prevent you from sharing authority.

At a minimum, a supervisor should delegate enough authority:

1. To get the work done
2. To allow key people to take initiative
3. To keep things going even in the absence of the supervisor

Authority emanates from the top position in the organizational structure and it is filtered through the chain of command. *Webster's Seventh New Collegiate Dictionary* defines "authority" as "power to influence or command thought, opinion or behavior." The security profession is built on a solid foundation of chain of command. The security supervisor must know how to effectively use his authority to achieve the desired results.

[14]Wanat, John A, Brown, John F., and Connin, Laurence C., *Hospital Security Guard Training Manual*, Springfield, Thomas, 1977, pp. 10-12.

MAINTAINING CONTROL

It is essential for a supervisor who manages others to maintain control. This can be accomplished by holding subordinates responsible for their actions while checking on the results of those actions.

A supervisor must, however, maintain a happy medium in controlling operations. The supervisor cannot afford to overshadow his employees nor can he afford to be so far removed that control is lost. Ideally, the supervisor must be kept informed through established feedback procedures. This can be accomplished through the use of: timely reports, be they daily, weekly or monthly; periodic staff meetings; and individualized sessions.

Remember to allow subordinates a certain degree of flexibility in carrying out assignments. It is not absolutely necessary for them to use the same methods as the supervisor. Allow subordinates, keeping within company policy, to do things their own way. It is the results that count, not the methods.

It is equally important for the supervisor to provide technical assistance to his subordinates. This assistance should be in the form of guidance and direction when the need arises. It should not be meddlesome interference. Remember, the supervisor's job is to plan, direct and coordinate the work of others. In this capacity, the supervisor should practice good communication techniques, making sure the subordinate understands the tasks at hand, the general procedures for accomplishing the tasks, and the time frame for reporting progress and final results.

Tips on Maintaining Control

- Provide technical assistance as the need arises
- Involve subordinates in the planning process
- Accept suggestions on ways and means of simplifying procedures
- Be fair
- Give credit where credit is due
- Clearly communicate what is expected of subordinates
- Provide subordinates with challenging assignments, but make certain it's within their ability to accomplish the task
- Establish procedures for soliciting feedback on progress

SELF-CONTROL

A security supervisor must maintain self-control at all times when dealing with subordinates. You cannot be in control if you let your emotions get the upper hand.

Although easier said than done, make an effort to practice self-control at all times. It is especially difficult to maintain self-control when someone else is noticeably angry and shouting. This is not to say that a supervisor cannot be firm and demonstrate strength in office. But a security supervisor should not get so angry that emotions override sound judgment.

Some suggestions for handling a difficult encounter:[15]

- Count to ten. Take time to think and compose yourself.
- If you remain calm, the other person will be more likely to calm down. Have you ever tried yelling at a person who is speaking in a soft, low voice?
- If the person won't calm down, and you feel you are losing your cool, say, "Let's think about this a while and talk about it a bit later."
- Sometimes it is better to just listen, letting the other person blow off steam and get it out of his system.
- If things really get bad, get up and walk away, saying, "Let's discuss this tomorrow when we have had more time to think about it objectively."

HANDLING DISCIPLINE PROBLEMS

Effectively handling discipline problems is a form of control. A security supervisor must know how to handle discipline problems lest he lose control of the department. Some tips to keep in mind when dealing with discipline problems are:

- Never criticize in public.
- Avoid reprimanding subordinates in front of others.
- Be consistent in handling discipline problems.
- Don't show favoritism.
- Discuss discipline situations in private with the concerned party. Talk things out. Let the party know where he stands in any given situation.
- Don't overlook violations. The time to take positive action is at the outset. Waiting until the situation gets critical is too late.

STAFF DEVELOPMENT

A good supervisor develops his staff's compentencies. Subordinates should be prepared to assume control. Staff development requires the supervisor teach management techniques to subordinates. Subordinates do not automatically acquire management skill; it has to be taught.

Good management techniques require supervisors to keep their subordinates informed. Provide them with the facts so that they can make wise decisions. The supervisor must, therefore, coach his subordinates. Coaching can be accomplished by:

---

[15]*Industrial Cooperative Training II*, Curriculum Guide, General Related Study Guides, Richmond, Virginia, 1976.

- Structured on-the-job training
- Encouraging questions from subordinates
- Providing in-house training
- Encouraging discussion
- Keeping subordinates involved
- Explaining the reasons behind an assignment

Supervisors frequently find themselves involved in many operational details, even though everything necessary for delegating responsibility appears to have been done. In spite of defining authority, delegating to competent individuals, spelling out the delegation, keeping control, and coaching, supervisors are still burdened with detailed work. Why?

Usually, they have failed to do one vital thing. They have refused to stand back and let the wheels turn.

Delegation cannot work unless subordinates are given some flexibility in getting things done their way. Supervisors must judge by results, not by methods.

People do not act the same way in every situation. Supervisors must be prepared to see things done differently from the way in which they themselves would do it, even though policies are well defined.

Of course, if subordinates stray too far from policy, supervisors need to bring them back in line.

Supervisors, however, should keep in mind that when they second-guess assistants, they risk destroying their self-confidence. Supervisors should replace assistants who do not run the department to their satisfaction or whose shortcomings cannot be overcome. But when results prove their effectiveness, it is good practice to avoid picking at each move they make.

DELEGATION, AUTHORITY, AND CONTROL CHECKLIST

YES NO

☐	☐	1.	I let others take care of the details.
☐	☐	2.	I get work done through people.
☐	☐	3.	I delegate sufficient authority and control to get the work done.
☐	☐	4.	I allow competent subordinates to perform in their own style rather than insist that they perform exactly as I would in carrying out the assignment.
☐	☐	5.	I let subordinates know exactly for what I am holding them responsible.
☐	☐	6.	I allow sufficient time to carry out a given assignment.
☐	☐	7.	I train subordinates to handle the department in my absence.
☐	☐	8.	I work out practices and procedures to get a job done.

YES NO

☐	☐	9.	I put procedures in writing.
☐	☐	10.	I spell out the responsibilities and authority for each subordinate and/or position.
☐	☐	11.	I hold subordinates responsible for their actions.
☐	☐	12.	I maintain a positive check on the results of my subordinates' actions.
☐	☐	13.	I keep informed on operations through continuous feedback.
☐	☐	14.	I keep subordinates informed.
☐	☐	15.	I provide subordinates with the facts they need to make decisions.
☐	☐	16.	I judge by results and not by methods.
☐	☐	17.	I don't second-guess subordinates.
☐	☐	18.	I avoid picking at each move a subordinate makes.
☐	☐	19.	I provide technical assistance to subordinates.
☐	☐	20.	I endeavor to strengthen the morale of my department.
☐	☐	21.	I reprimand privately.
☐	☐	22.	I use criticism sparingly and constructively.

BIBLIOGRAPHY

"Delegating Work and Responsibility," Small Business Administration, Management Aids #191, September 1967., SBA, Washington, D.C.

Drucher, Peter F., *The Practice of Management*, Harper & Row, New York, 1954.

Dyer, Frederick C., *Executives Guide to Handling People*, Prentice Hall Inc., Englewood Cliffs, New Jersey, 1958, 16th printing 1970.

"How to Write a Job Description," Management Aid No. 171. Small Business Administration. SBA, Washington, D.C.

Moore, Franklin G., *Management Organization and Practices*, McGraw Hill Book Co., New York, 1961.

"Pointers for Developing Your Top Assistant," Small Marketers Aid No. 101. Small Business Administration. SBA, Washington, D.C.

Schleh, Edward C., *Management by Results*, Mc Graw Hill Book Co., New York, 1961.

7

Complaints and Grievances

Important responsibilities of a security supervisor are receiving, evaluating, investigating, recording and taking action on complaints and grievances.

When an officer takes the time to make a formal complaint to you, remember that it took courage to do so, and it is of great importance to that person, no matter how trivial, it might seem to you.

An officer can become irritated over a work schedule and develop a minor complaint about the situation. A security officer needs to be able to release his frustration concerning working the evening shift. A sympathetic ear about the evening work, even though you might not be able to change the situation for some time, will often satisfy the irritated officer, who wants and needs to verbally express his displeasure.

Failing to listen to the officer's complaint can lead to pent-up emotions. This can, and often does, result in the officer filing a formal complaint and/or grievance against the company. The "grievance," real or unfounded, can often be avoided if the supervisor exercises a few common practices.

- Listen to what your subordinates have to say. If a real problem exists, take corrective action.
- Never belittle an officer or ridicule him about his complaint and/or gripe. What is imaginary or unreal to you may not be perceived the same way by others.
- Gather all the facts concerning a complaint, weigh the facts, then take appropriate and decisive action.
- Always adhere to company policy. Explain the reasons behind your decisions and orders.
- Keep subordinates informed. Let them know how they are progressing. Also, explain in detail any changes in company policy or decisions.

COMPLAINTS/GRIEVANCES

When handling complaints or grievances from security officers, make sure officers can talk face to face with their supervisor. These conversations should be casual and nonthreatening. The supervisor should be aware of the officers' needs, know what motivates them and, above all, understand them. Most officers will usually react in a positive manner during the conference possibly stating outright their dissatisfaction or problems. Management, during the communication process for complaints for or grievances, must listen to what is being passed to them by their supervisory personnel.

Many areas of complaints and grievances from security officers fall into the following areas:

- The job is not understood or made clear
- Lack of particular skills for the job
- Lack of training in the job to make the officer more proficient
- Standards are too rigid
- Unrealistic demands made by "higher-ups"
- Enforcing unenforceable rules or regulations
- Complying with unenforceable rules or regulations
- Schedules
- Conflicting orders of supervisors
- Lack of necessary information
- Lack of decision-making by supervisors or high management
- Unable to grow within the department or company
- Unchallenging work, i.e., stuck on a monotonous post day after day
- Undersupervision—indicating the work is not too important
- Oversupervision—indicating self-initiated work performance by the officer would not be worthwhile
- Absence or lack of recognition for performance—indicating that sometimes mediocre performance receives the same recognition as top performance; the top performers wonder if their performance is worthwhile

A supervisor should use all means possible to cut down the number of complaints or grievances. They must continually keep their ear to the ground to possibly head off what could turn into a complaint or grievance.

Some departments use surveys when face to face meetings are not held as aforementioned. The results of a survey which has been structured right will usually give a superficial indication of attitudes, needs, or complaints an officer might want to express.

The results of a questionnaire or survey must always be examined very carefully. They often indicate that you might have failed to allow an officer to communicate any complaints or grievances. Overall, surveys will also give you some knowledge of why morale is low or high.

PITFALLS TO AVOID

The following pitfalls should be avoided, since they will lead to gripes, complaints and finally grievances.

- Don't show favoritism

- Don't criticize in front of other officers
- Don't assume credit for subordinates' ideas
- Don't keep answers to yourself
- Don't delay in settling a complaint or grievance
- Don't rely on memory—record the facts
- Don't pass the buck
- Don't antagonize others
- Don't be sarcastic to officers
- Don't needle officers

HOW TO HANDLE A PROBLEM[16]

1. Get the facts
   - Review the record
   - Find out what rules and plant customs apply
   - Talk with individuals concerned
   - Get opinions and feelings

   Be sure you have the whole story.

2. Weigh and decide
   - Fit the facts together
   - Consider their bearing on each other
   - Check practices and policies
   - What possible actions are there?
   - Consider effect on individuals, groups and production

   Don't jump to conclusions!

3. Take action
   - Are you going to handle this yourself?
   - Do you need help in handling?
   - Should you refer this to your superior?
   - Watch the timing of your action

   Don't pass the buck!

4. Check results
   - How soon will you follow up?
   - How often will you need to check?
   - Watch for changes in output, attitudes, and relationships

   Did your action help production?

GRIEVANCE PROCEDURE

A grievance can be defined as a claimed breach, misinterpretation or improper application of the terms of an agreement (contractual grievance); or a claimed violation, misinterpretation, or misapplication of rules or regulations, existing

---

[16]Donald F. Favreau, "Fire Service Management," *Fire Engineering*, 1969, pp. 65-66.

policy, or orders, applicable to the agency or department which employs the grievant affecting the terms and conditions of employment and which are not included above (non-contractual grievance).[17]

The grievance procedure assures prompt and equitable solutions to problems arising from the administration of a contractual agreement, or other conditions of employment.

The supervisor should be aware that the subordinate is entitled to use the grievance procedure without fear of being coerced or intimidated. The subordinate should not suffer any reprisal as a direct or indirect result of initiating a grievance procedure. As a matter of fact, a well-planned grievance procedure will settle most grievances in a fair and equitable manner.

Objectives of a Grievance Procedure

The basic objectives of a grievance procedure are:
• To provide a forum for employees to be heard
• To provide an equitable means for both management and employees to settle real or imaginary problems
• To provide a decision or response within a reasonable time frame
• To provide for arbitration procedures when an impasse occurs.

The Supervisor's Role in the Grievance Procedure

As an agent of management, the security supervisor is responsible for implementing company policy, procedures, rules and regulations. In this respect, the supervisor is also the individual who must deal with employee grievances. The following procedures will assist the supervisor in handling grievances:

• Maintain an open door policy. Listen to the employee without interruptions and maintain a composed attitude.
• Solicit details; get the facts. Ask questions without antagonizing the employee.
• Be objective and fair in your investigation procedures. Look at all sides of the issue.
• Record your facts and information on paper. Don't trust your memory to recall all the issues and facts surrounding the grievance.
• When in doubt, consult with other supervisors and/or your immediate superior. Consultation will reinforce your decision or point out something you missed. In any case, consultation is smart, not dumb.
• Take action within the given time limits.

[17]New Jersey Civil Service Association and New Jersey State Employees Association—Professional Unit Agreement, 1979.

- Maintain company policy. Render a decision for or against the employee that is consistent with company policy and past practice. Always explain the reasons behind the policy.
- Process appeals promptly. If the employee is dissatisfied with your decision, the grievance may go to the next step. Your responsibility is to forward the appeal, accompanied by your written disposition on the matter. Forward dates, facts, summary, and outcome promptly to the next level.

ARBITRATION

If the grievance has not been satisfactorily resolved, it is submitted to arbitration. This is the final step in the grievance process. The arbitrator conducts a hearing to determine the facts and render a decision in writing to the parties. The arbitrator does not have the power to add to, subtract from, or modify the provisions of the union agreement or any written company policy.

The arbitrator confines himself to the precise issue submitted for arbitration and has no authority to determine any other issues. Nor can he submit observations or declarations of opinion which are not essential in reaching the determination. The decision or award of the arbitrator is final and binding.

DISSATISFACTION PROCEDURES (A Sample)[18]

Policy:

All employees have full opportunity to air dissatisfaction and concerns. It is company policy to thoroughly investigate all incidents of employee dissatisfaction. Where there is a legitimate reason for complaint, which appears to arise from a condition of employment, every effort shall be made toward rectification.

Employees are encouraged to present complaints and problems without fear of penalty. This policy, as adopted, will be implemented in full accord with the spirit of the code of employee relations.

Implementation:

Formal Complaint Procedure:

Step # 1—An employee having a complaint about any condition of employment may present the complaint to his immediate supervisor. The supervisor shall make known to the complainant his determination within 48

[18]Rahway Hospital, Personnel Policies, 1975.

hours (weekends excluded). If the decision is unsatisfactory to the employee, he may then initiate Step # 2.

Step # 2—An employee whose complaint or problem has not been resolved to his satisfaction by the immediate supervisor may present the matter to his department head. The department head shall investigate and discuss with the immediate supervisor the action taken to date. The department head will make known to the complainant his own determination within 48 hours (weekends excluded). If the employee remains of the opinion that the matter is still unresolved, he may proceed to take Step # 3.

Note: In those departments where the department head acts as the immediate supervisor the employee proceeds directly from Step # 1 to Step # 3.

Step # 3—The employee may request that the matter be subsequently reviewed by the personnel department. The department head and employee shall discuss the complaint with the Director of Personnel, who shall endeavor to resolve the issue to the satisfaction of all concerned. If the employee is still not satisfied he may proceed to initiate the final step.

Step # 4—The personnel department requests that the employee present the complaint in writing. The complaint in written form shall be transmitted to the Director accompanied by a written report and findings as adjudicated by the personnel department and as required to be submitted. The Director's decision shall be final and binding upon all parties.

Note: If complainant employee is connected with one of the departments on the organizational chart under the Assistant Director, procedure requires that employee's written complaint accompanied by the findings of the personnel department be first relayed to the Assistant Director for his review and due consultation with all principals. The decision of the Assistant Director may be appealed by the employee if, in the latter's opinion, the matter still remains unresolved. The Assistant Director's findings in written form accompanied by all other written summations relative to the grievance are, in this instance, then forwarded to the Director as outlined in Step # 4.

HANDLING COMPLAINTS AND GRIEVANCES—CHECKLIST

YES	NO		
☐	☐	1.	I endeavor to keep complaints from becoming grievances.
☐	☐	2.	I am willing to listen to my subordinates' problems.
☐	☐	3.	I don't ignore a subordinates' complaint.
☐	☐	4.	I communicate with my subordinates and always explain why something has to be done or why something cannot be done because of company policy.
☐	☐	5.	I seek to get at the root of a subordinates' complaint.
☐	☐	6.	I talk to my subordinates and investigate the reasons behind a complaint.

YES NO

☐ ☐ 7. I endeavor to ascertain the fact or fiction behind a sub-ordinate's complaint.

☐ ☐ 8. I weigh all the facts before I make a decision or take further action on a subordinates' complaint.

☐ ☐ 9. I take prompt corrective action on mild irritations.

☐ ☐ 10. I am fair in all my dealings with subordinates.

☐ ☐ 11. I do not show favoritism.

☐ ☐ 12. I avoid reacting negatively to a subordinates' complaint.

☐ ☐ 13. I listen attentively to a subordinates' complaint.

☐ ☐ 14. I endeavor to provide fulfilling experiences for the chronic complainer.

☐ ☐ 15. I provide a forum for subordinates to be heard.

☐ ☐ 16. I endeavor to provide an answer to a subordinates' question within a reasonable time frame.

☐ ☐ 17. I investigate the facts to a complaint.

☐ ☐ 18. I take decisive action after gathering all the facts on a given situation.

☐ ☐ 19. I am impartial in my dealings with subordinates.

☐ ☐ 20. I never try to cover-up a complaint or grievance.

☐ ☐ 21. I maintain my composure when dealing with a complaint/grievance.

☐ ☐ 22. I seek a consultation with other supervisors and/or superiors in handling difficult situations.

BIBLIOGRAPHY

Beletz, Elaine E., "Some Pointers For Grievance Handlers," *Supervisor Nurse*, pp. 12-14, August, 1977.

Establishment of an Employee Grievance Procedure, American Hospital Association, Chicago, Ill., 1975.

Byrd, Stephen F.: *Front Line Supervisor's Labor Relations Handbook*, National Foremen's Institute, Waterford, Conn., 1978.

The Supervisor's Role in Handling Complaints and Grievances, International Association Chiefs of Police, 11J1-11J8.

"Treating Complaints, *Dynamic Supervision*, Bureau of Business Practice, Waterford, Conn., #487, August 10, 1978.

"Discipline and Grievances: Everyday Problems in the Plant and Office,"—*Personnel Management Policies and Practices*, Prentice-Hall Inc., 1971.

8

Training Skill Development

Until recently, very little attention and effort was paid to the training function of security officers. The philosophy and practice of training security personnel at all levels is finally coming to the forefront. Greater and greater emphasis is being placed on upgrading the knowledge and skills of the security officer.

There are still no uniform training standards across the country for entry level security officers. There is, however, more and more inservice training taking place within security departments, within professional associations, and within higher education institutions. A few models will be presented to familiarize you with the technical content of some basic security training for security officers and security supervisors.

The emphasis of this unit, however, is not on the technical aspect of the security field, rather it is focused on training methodology and training techniques.

COLLEGIATE SECURITY TRAINING PROGRAM

A ten-week, twenty-hour basic security training program was initiated in 1973 at the Center for Occupational Education, Jersey City State College. This program was initiated specifically for security personnel at a local hospital, who expressed a need for training and who were frustrated in finding an institution or agency that was willing to train their security officers. The program that was tailored for them developed into a regularly scheduled program offered to security personnel throughout the state. The curriculum consists of two-hour sessions in Fire Prevention and Inspection, Fire Evacuation and Extinguishment, Laws of Arrest - Search and Seizure, Patrol Functions, Public Relations, Preventive Security, Reports, Report Writing, Bomb Procedures, and Safety.

IAHS BASIC TRAINING PROGRAM

The International Association for Hospital Security (IAHS) has developed a forty-hour basic security training program that has met with great success throughout the country. That program is outlined on page 85.

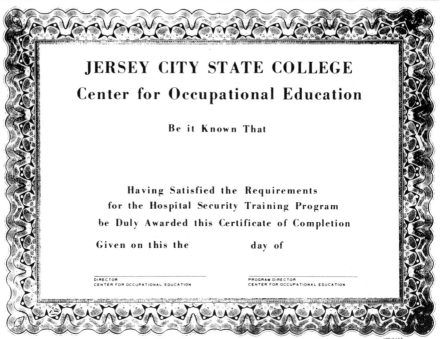

Figure 8-1.

Figure 8-2.

FIGURE 8-1 and FIGURE 8-2.   Two types of certificates issued by Jersey City State College in their security training programs. (Courtesy of Jersey City State College.)

Topic	Hours
Fire Prevention	2
Fire Control	2
Report and Report Writing	3
Patrol Functions	3
Organization	
a. Security as a service organization	1
b. Hospital Organization	1
Relations	
a. Public	½
b. Community	½
c. Labor	1
Laws of Arrest/Search/Seizure	2
Hospital Safety	2
Investigation/Interviews	2
Narcotics and Dangerous Drugs	2
Disaster Control	2
Hospital Operations	
a. Nursing	1
b. Business office	1
c. Ancillary services	1
d. Food service	1
e. Pharmacy	1
f. Hospital vulnerabilities	1
Bomb Procedures	2
Physical Security Controls	1
Law Enforcement Liaison	1
Alarms	1
Lock and Keys	1
Equipment Usage/Maintenance	1
Courtroom Procedures	1
Disturbances	
a. Civil	1
b. Handling the patient, visitor, employee	1

SUPERVISORY DEVELOPMENT STANDARD FOR HOSPITAL SECURITY OFFICERS

Another professional program of the International Association for Hospital Security is the Supervisory Development Standard Program. This training program is designed for line personnel to develop a better understanding of the principles of supervision. The twenty-hour training program is formal classroom or formal demonstration instruction. The subjects include Training, Skill Development, Self-Improvement, Leadership Development, Authority and Control, Handling Complaints and Grievances, Effective Communication, Supervisory Responsibilities, Community and Human Relations, Managerial Skill for Supervisory Personnel, Time Management, Safety Attitude Development, Motivation, and Ethics.

The American Society for Industrial Security (ASIS) offers a Certified Protection Professional Program, CPP, which recognizes security practitioners who have demonstrated a high level of competence by passing professional examinations, and by demonstrating high levels of performance based on personal experience data. This comprehensive program is highlighted in the Appendix.

TRAINING

Learning is a life-long process. We learn by everything we do. We learn by observing, reading, listening, and doing. We learn either formally or informally. The informal process is normally unstructured. We learn like a child who, as an infant, observes and picks up everything that goes on in his environment. The infant learns to speak simply by listening and doing.

The formal learning process is highly structured. It is organized in such a way as to provide guidance and direction to learners, so that they can master what is being taught. Structured learning goes from the known to the unknown, it goes from the easy to the complex. It requires a transfer of knowledge, proceeding from a point already known and applying it to a new situation.

Training is a formal learning process. The dictionary defines training as a form of instruction, discipline, or drill that can be used to teach or to make someone proficient. Effective training is a method by which someone can learn new skills or improve upon already developed skills.

Security training is important if you expect officers to do their jobs properly. A well-organized training program prepares officers to do a good job efficiently and safely. Training programs are needed for new officers, for introducing new equipment and processes, for retraining an officer in new techniques, for upgrading officers' skills, and for improving officers' performance.

How to Train

Training programs should be based on clearly defined training objectives. What is it you want the security officer to learn? What do you expect them to achieve by the training process? What methods can you use to measure the effectiveness of the training? Every training program should be able to answer these three questions. Every security supervisor is responsible for training his subordinates. A knowledge of how to train is essential. It is not essential for the security supervisor to have a degree in teaching. It is important, however, that the supervisor have some background in methods of training, as well as a sincere desire to help his staff. Adhering to the following training tips will help the supervisor become an effective trainer.

- Establish rapport with the trainees
- Encourage the trainees to participate; let them ask questions freely
- Know the trainees' names
- Be aware of any individual differences
- Keep attendance records
- Effectively use audio-visual equipment and training aides
- Make the classroom environment pleasant
- Thoroughly prepare your subject matter
- Vary your teaching techniques
- Display a sense of humor
- Place the trainees at ease
- Prepare detailed lesson plans
- Explain fully each step of the training process
- Refrain from sarcasm in the class
- Be clear in your instructions
- Stay on the subject
- Thoroughly cover all the material in your lesson
- Teach at the class's level
- Cultivate a sense of individual responsibilities
- Summarize the key points

METHODS OF INSTRUCTION

There are many methods to use in training and instruction. Listed in this section are those most commonly used.

Lecture Method

The lecture method is the most commonly known method of instruction. It is most effective when used to arouse interest in an area or to set the stage for further discussion. The lecture method is best used for large audiences, where a great deal of material has to be covered in a very short period of time. This method, however, is not the ideal method of instruction. It is one-way communication, and does not allow free discussion. Further, it does not hold the listener's interest for long. The lecture method is best used for short periods of time where complex material has to be presented. You should use other methods of instruction, and allow time for questions and answers.

Discussion

This method succeeds when it is geared to small groups of 20 to 25 people. It should be controlled by a leader who is highly structured. The discussion method is also known as the conference, or seminar, method. The participants tackle a problem or a set of problems and have an opportunity to exchange ideas and information. It allows for divergent points of view. Everyone has an opportunity to participate. The discussion method can fall apart if the discussion leader does not keep the participants on the subject. It is best used to resolve problems after a lecture or an audio-visual demonstration.

Demonstration

The demonstration method is in reality "show and tell." The participants have an opportunity to see as well as to hear about the subject. It is a "how-to" method. When it is well-planned and skillfully executed, it is most effective. The demonstration method requires a great deal of preparation to insure that all is in readiness and in proper order before class begins. It requires that you break the subject down to steps, arranged in logical order. Failing to provide a good demonstration will result in poor understanding of the subject presented.

Dramatization

Dramatization provides students with an opportunity to participate. Situations are created and participants are named to act out the parts. Dramatization must be based on clearly defined issues. These issues must be understood by all the participants if the dramatization is to be effective. Dramatization is often an unplanned demonstration. Certain guidelines, however, must be used in order for it to be effective.

- People must be at ease.
- A cooperative atmosphere must exist.
- Individuals should volunteer to participate.
- Allow the actors a few minutes to discuss what they are going to do to dramatize the issue.
- Have the audience refrain from interruptions until the dramatization is ended.
- After the dramatization is ended, have the entire group discuss the issue in detail.

The dramatization issue should have a direct influence on a real on-the-job situation for it to be effective.

Role-Playing

Role-playing is similar to the dramatization method. Participants act out real-life situations. Role-playing has participants act out how they feel. The participants behave according to their feelings. The outcome of a role-playing situation is not predetermined. It depends on how the actors behave during their role-playing. Role-playing is primarily used to help individuals understand human behavior. It is also used to help the participants improve interactive skills, that is, the skills involved in working with people.

Case Studies

Case studies are problem-oriented. They deal with the report of a real situation that has occurred. Or, they can deal with a simulated situation that can be related to a real situation. This method provides information about a particular situation. Participants are given an opportunity to decide the extent of the problem and provide solutions to the situation.

Panel

Bringing together two or more qualified individuals, who will discuss an assigned topic or subject, is a panel. Panel discussion is often followed by a question and answer period, where the audience has an opportunity to ask pertinent questions of the experts on the panel.

Simulation

Simulation imitates the behavior of a system. For example, a mock device representing hydraulic pumpers on fire engines. Simulators are classroom tools, controlled by the instructor, which put the trainee through a series of exercises and initiate problems that can be corrected. Simulation examines problems not often subject to direct experimentation. Simulation exercises have been used to train astronauts and pilots so that they can properly handle their space capsules or airplanes. Simulation parallels real life or actual conditions, thus affording the participant the opportunity to make a decision without incurring an actual risk.

ON-THE-JOB TRAINING

All the previous methods centered around group instruction in a classroom setting. On-the-job training, however, takes place at the trainee's workplace. It is individualized instruction. The cooperating supervisor assists the new employee in understanding the job that they are performing. The employee assigned to train the new person continues to perform his normal duties in addition to assisting the new employee. The trainee works alongside the cooperating supervisor and asks questions as need arises. The on-the-job training supervisor takes the initiative to point out what they are doing and the proper method and procedure for doing it. There are four recognized steps to providing on-the-job instruction:

1. Prepare the trainee on the job.
2. Present the entire subject to the trainee.
3. Have the trainee repeat the performance.
4. Conduct a follow-up.

It is essential that the security trainer understand these techniques of instruction so that the trainee can be adequately prepared to do the job.

Prepare the Trainee on the Job

Place the individual at ease. Determine what the trainee already knows about the job. Explain in detail the subject to be covered and why it is important. Get the trainee interested in learning the job, so that he can do it effectively and safely. Provide the trainee with a complete overview of the subject area. Break down the subject into small segments and then take the trainee from the simple to the complex or from the known to the unknown.

Present the Entire Subject to the Trainee

Demonstrate the proper procedures for carrying out the duty or assignment. Stress the key points. Illustrate one important step at a time. Give the trainee an opportunity to repeat back the instructions so that the trainee can tell the trainer, in his own words, what was learned. Remember that language should be simple and precise, so the listener or the trainee understands what is being said. Be cautious about presenting too much at one time. This is known as overload. Present the instruction to the trainee in amounts that can be grasped and mastered at one time.

Have the Trainee Repeat the Performance

After the instruction has been given to the trainee, require him to perform the job under close supervision. The trainee should explain in detail each key point as he goes along. Make sure that the trainee understands every facet of what he is performing. At this time, the trainer should correct any errors made by the trainee.

Conduct a Follow-Up

Once the trainee has demonstrated that he can perform the given task or assignment, the trainee should be placed on his own. He should be able to come back for assistance at any point. It becomes the responsibility of the trainer to occasionally review certain techniques. The trainee should be encouraged to ask questions about any phase that is unclear. Most importantly, the trainee should be kept abreast of his progress. The follow-up is usually conducted two weeks after the trainee has demonstrated an awareness of the proper procedures. Following the two-week follow-up, a thirty-day follow-up and a six-month follow-up are in order. Retraining should be provided as the need arises. Every employee, new or old, should be trained or retrained from time to time.

ORGANIZING THE TRAINING CLASS

Formal in-service training programs should be provided frequently for officers. The class size should be about 15-25 officers. Classes exceeding 25 become unruly and do not allow a great deal of communication or questions and answers. If the group exceeds 25, consider splitting the group into two or more classes.

The training should be in a room which is well ventilated, well lighted, and away from any distracting noises. The meeting place should be one that is attractive, clean, and conducive to learning. Seating accommodations should be such that the participants can take notes. The meeting room should have a chalkboard, chalk, and erasers. The seats should be comfortable and the trainees should be able to adequately hear and see the instructor at the front of the room.

USE OF AUDIO-VISUAL AIDS

Appropriate, well-planned audio-visual aids are essential to any training program. The audio-visual aids should not be the sole training device—they are aids that supplement the instructor. Pre-planning is necessary to decide which audio-visual aids suit the message. The aids should be appropriate to the event or conditions under which you are using them. Figure 8-3 suggests visual selections for the audience size and event.

QUALITIES OF INSTRUCTORS

The following eleven qualities should be demonstrated by the instructor when conducting training sessions:

Visual aids	Size of audience	Advantages	Disadvantages
Chalkboard	Recommended for 35 participants and under	Easy to use; requires little or no advance preparation; colored chalk adds variety and interest	Often difficult to read from any dis-distance; lines are often too thin for good visibility; it becomes messy
Flip Charts	35 participants or under	Quality visuals can be prepared well in advance with drawings and lettering; individual sheets can reveal a point at a time	Cumbersome to manipulate; thin paper often requires an intersheet
Slides	Large groups	Very versatile; depicts many things well; easy to obtain at low cost	Requires room be darkened; projector and screen must be on hand
Overhead	Medium to large groups	Can be prepared ahead of time; charts and graphs can be viewed; trainer can write on them during projection	Overhead projector must be available; need large screen angled to remove keystoning
Motion Pictures	Large groups	Films can be rented or purchased on every conceivable subject; they complement any presentation provided they are short	Room must be darkened; screen and movie projector(s) must be available; projectors have been known to occasionally tear up the film and bulbs burn out at any given time
Videotapes	Limited to small audience who can view a T.V. screen	Great deal of flexibility; low cost in preparing one's own message	Unless the projection equipment is available the speaker must carry T.V. and videotaping equipment with him; limits audience to a small group who can view T.V. monitors

FIGURE 8-3. Suggested uses of visual aids.

1. Interest in trainees
2. Mastery of the subject matter
3. Pleasing personality
4. Fairness
5. Desire to teach
6. Ability to be well organized
7. Ability to break down the subject into easily understood components
8. Desire to be helpful
9. Have a wide range of information
10. Demonstrate enthusiasm
11. Have a diverse presentation of material

LESSON PLANS

A lesson plan (or training plan) is a detailed outline of all major and minor points necessary for the instructor to teach. In addition to outlining the material to be taught, it should suggest sequences, media and procedures. The lesson plan should deal with a single subject. It presupposes that the ideas and procedures can be mastered by the trainees in the allotted time.

The purposes of the lesson should be clearly and concisely stated. The lesson must be logically structured so that it takes the trainees through the steps that are know for the desired objectives. All essential training aids should be listed.

A major section to the training plan is the introduction, which is a written description paraphrasing the objectives stated in the heading. It is meant to draw attention to the class. A detailed explanation follows in topical outline form. The main points to be covered are listed along with subtopics. Supporting information is written in singular words or brief phrases. Notes to the instructor are inserted wherever needed. The last part of the outline is the summary, which consists of a series of questions and statements. The questions check the key points. Statements may be reemphasized.

GOALS OF TRAINING

- To improve the performance of employees
- To orient new employees to their job
- To assist employees by training them to perform their present tasks better
- To prepare employees for newly developed or modified jobs
- To prepare employees for promotions
- To reduce accidents and increase safety practices
- To improve employee attitudes

- To train employees so they can help teach new employees in an expansion program
- To upgrade the profession as a whole
- To provide the trainee with the most up-to-date information

OUTCOMES OF TRAINING

- It increases efficiency
- It improves employees' work attitudes
- It improves morale
- It increases judgment
- It develops pride
- It reduces turnover
- It increases job satisfaction
- It promotes safety
- It promotes professionalism
- It generates a feeling of belonging

TRAINING CHECKLIST

YES NO

1. I use a manual of instruction, including job instruction sheets.
2. I have a prepared lesson plan.
3. I issue trainees an outline of the training program.
4. I effectively use outside textbooks and other printed materials.
5. I arrange for sufficient seating and writing surfaces for the trainees.
6. I maintain a complete record on the progress of each trainee.
7. I know each trainee by their first name.
8. I test trainees on the knowledge and skills acquired.
9. I periodically follow up the trainee to determine the long-range effects of the training.
10. I award certificates to trainees who complete the training.
11. I effectively use training aids wherever possible.
12. I review all films before showing them.
13. I use test results to determine weak points in my teaching.
14. I cover the material in each lesson.
15. I clearly outline the objectives of each lesson.
16. I summarize each lesson.
17. I refrain from using sarcasm in my classroom teaching.
18. I provide a variety of teaching methods.
19. I use language that is easily understood by my trainees.
20. I make assignments that are clear and achievable.

BIBLIOGRAPHY

Accident Prevention Manual for Industrial Operations, 7th edition, National Safety Council, Chicago, Illinois, 1974. Safety training, Chapter 9, pp. 196-215.

Berry, D.R.: *Effective Training: A Guide for the Company Instructor*, International Textbook Company, Scranton, Pennsylvania, 1969.

Checklist for Developing a Training Program Small Business Administration, Management Aids #186, Washington, D.C., 1967.

Instructor Training Course, New Jersey State Police Training Bureau, Sea Girt, New Jersey.

Lesson Plan Construction, U.S. Army Signal Center and School, Ft. Monmouth, New Jersey, Itlt-13-IS-1.

Police Reference Book, Supervisors Training Function, The International Association of Chief of Police Professional Standards, Unit 11F, Garthersburg, MD., 1974.

Training, Portfolios 1 through 12, Bureau of Business Practices, 1965.

9

Safety Attitude Development

Security supervisors often have the responsibility of instilling safety conscious-ness into their subordinates. The ideal time to begin this process is as soon as a new person is hired. If people are trained to have a positive safety attitude early, they will think and act safely.

Merely telling people to behave safely will not motivate them to change their unsafe behavior patterns. An example is the automotive industry where seat belts are required to be installed in all new cars. Even though the general public is informed of the advantages of using seat belts, the majority of drivers neglect to "buckle up for safety." Adding warning lights and ignition lock-out devices to automobiles did not substantially change things. People simply found ways to disengage these safety precaution devices.

The airline industry requires its passengers to fasten their seat belts during take-off and landing in rough weather and during emergency situations. Most people, as a matter of habit, fasten their seat belts when they board an airplane. This is especially true of those who are accustomed to flying. The commercial airline industry introduced the seat belt safety habit early to its passengers while the automobile industry apparently introduced the safety device much too late for it to be widely accepted. This analogy supports the proposition that habits formed early, good or bad, are hard to break.

An important aspect of teaching safety awareness to subordinates is for the supervisor to demonstrate, by constant example, proper safety procedures in carrying out assignments. You cannot expect subordinates to conform to positive safety standards when you neglect to behave safely. A subordinate cannot take a supervisor's "No Smoking" order seriously if the supervisor smokes in unauthorized areas.

Instilling safety consciousness into subordinates is no simple task. It takes time, effort and constant positive reinforcement. The subject of safety is not something that can be discussed today and forgotten tomorrow. Building positive safety attitudes in your subordinates requires constant attention and repetition. Constant reminders will assist subordinates in thinking, acting and working safely.

Warnings, alone, appear to be of little value in instilling safety awareness in our subordinates. Warnings certainly do prevent illness, accident or injury. Does the warning on a pack of cigarettes, "Warning: The Surgeon General Has Determined That Cigarette Smoking is Dangerous To Your Health," keep many people from smoking? Does the warning sign above the mechanic's garage door, "Do not enter this work area" keep customers from entering the area where mechanics have cars on lifts? Do we like to be told, "Drive carefully, now" as we enter a car to go somewhere? Do people react positively to warnings such as "Watch yourself?" Such admonitions may even cause some people to react negatively.

A valid safety program can help prevent accidents. It requires, however, that every person, from the highest ranking individual of the management team to the newest employee within the organization, think safety. It is a fallacy to believe that an establishment is safe because it has complied with existing state or federal government safety regulations. Warning signs and machine safety guards are not effective if the employees do not have the proper safety attitude and training.

SAFETY TRAINING

Safety training, through a well-planned safety program, appears to be an essential element in developing safe working habits. Security supervisors should provide their subordinates with on-the-job safety training, formal safety training programs, safety demonstrations, individualized safety talks, bulletin board displays, and employee safety meetings.

It is your responsibility to insure that all new subordinates are given proper safety training on the job. Accompany new security officers on routine patrol, pointing out safety hazards that should be reported, such as "no smoking" violations, cracked walking surfaces, defective electrical wiring, broken glass and items on floors that can cause slips and falls, blocked exits, or faulty fire extinguishers and equipment. Explain the proper procedures for reporting unsafe conditions in detail.

Formal Safety Training Programs

The responsibility for arranging formal in-house training programs for subordinates rests with the training supervisor. Formal training programs should consist of a combination of lectures, demonstrations, films, and reading material which thoroughly acquaints the new security officer with all safety aspects associated with their position.

In addition to regularly scheduled in-house training programs, formal training programs can take place through association workshops and college program's. Formal training programs should be used to introduce employee's management's safety regulations and procedures, to instill safety awareness as a habit, to identify proper safety methods of working, and to acquaint employees with new equipment and techniques.

Safety Demonstrations

There are a host of individuals and groups who are willing to demonstrate the proper safety techniques associated with their line of work or with their line of products.

For fire safety, the local fire department is usually more than eager to demonstrate the safety procedures for extinguishing small fires, using the appropriate fire extinguisher on a fire, evacuating a building, and conducting a fire safety inspection.

Manufacturers usually have trained technicians who are equally eager to demonstrate the safety features of their products.

First-aid squads and organizations such as the American Red Cross Association provide safety demonstrations and classes on how to administer emergency first aid, transport injured victims, and provide emergency disaster assistance.

Individualized Safety Talks

Since safety is a subject that should be given constant attention, it is wise to schedule individual safety talks with subordinates on a routine basis. This procedure provides the security supervisor with the opportunity to review the subordinate's accident record. It affords both parties the opportunity to ask questions that might not be brought out in the open during a group meeting. Individual problems relating to poor safety habits can be discussed while solutions can be arrived at for positive safety behavior.

Bulletin Board Displays

A positive reinforcement to all of the preceding approaches is to place appropriate safety posters on employee bulletin boards as well as in other conspicuous places. Simple, right to the point, posters and safety displays act as nonthreatening constant reminders to think, talk, and practice safety. A specific safety theme can be highlighted each month. For example, October is Fire Safety Month; November can be devoted to Good Housekeeping for Safety; December can stress Electrical Safety; January could be devoted to Positive Safety Attitude Modification. The National Safety Council has hundreds of inexpensive posters that the supervisor can order throughout the year.

Staff Safety Meetings

Periodic safety meetings should be conducted to discuss a specific safety topic.

Meetings of this nature should be routinely scheduled well in advance, so the staff can come prepared to intelligently discuss the scheduled topic. In this regard, the supervisor should come prepared with a statement of purpose, hand-out materials on the subject, and a determination to limit discussion to the specific topic of the day. Provide ample time for questions and answers. Plans for future meetings should be made before the staff safety meeting is brought to a conclusion. The supervisor should appoint a recorder who will maintain a record of these meetings. Figure 9-1 is an example of a brief form which summarizes the most important points discussed at a safety meeting. A copy should be distributed to those who attended the meeting as well as to other interested parties.

SAFETY INSPECTIONS

Since safe conditions depend on diligent vigilance for possible hazards and on immediate remedial action, routine inspections are one of the most important aspects of a successful safety program.

A checklist becomes an essential tool in performing a self-inspection of your facility. Keep in mind that although standardized checklists are useful, a customized list that meets your particular facility's needs is essential.

Using the checklist, you or a designated representative make periodic walk through inspections to identify problem areas so that appropriate corrective action may be taken.

Safety Inspection Guidelines[19]

An effective safety inspection depends on several factors. The individual or safety surveillance team must:

1.   Be selective. Coverage of all safety aspects in one tour of a department is difficult, if not impossible. Therefore, an inspector might check for basic safety the first time, for improvement of operations the second time, for training needs the third, and so on.
2.   Know what to look for. The more a supervisor or safety committee member knows about a job and each worker's responsibilities, the better an observer he will be.
3.   Practice observing. The more often a person makes a conscious effort to observe, the more he will see each time. Like all skills, observation improves with practice.
4.   Keep an open mind. The inspector must avoid judging facts in advance.

[19]Reprinted with permission, from *Safety Guide for Health Care Institutions*, a joint publication of the American Hospital Association and the National Safety Council, pp. 109-110.

RECORD OF SAFETY MEETING

Date: _____

Topic:_____

Short description of topic outcomes: _____

_____

_____

List hand-out materials:_____

_____

_____

Staff Attending:

_____   _____

_____   _____

_____   _____

Date of next meeting: _____

Topic(s) to be discussed _____

_____

FIGURE 9-1. Record of safety meeting.

He must not deny a fact, no matter what conclusion it may seem to force. He must keep his mind open until he has all the facts, then act accordingly.

5. Go beyond general impressions. A clean laboratory or pharmacy, or a careful routine, may still contain hidden hazards.

6. Guard against habit and familiarity. Asking the basic questions who, what, where, when, why, and how often will uncover the real meaning of a situation.

7. Record observations systematically. All notes should be dated, with space for comment on the action taken and its results. The notebook can serve both as a reminder and as a record of progress.

8. Prepare a checklist. A systematic check for litter, obstructions, handling of flammables, condition of fire-fighting equipment, and so forth, will uncover tangible problems that can be corrected.

9. Most important, set a good example.

Figure 9-2 shows an inspection checklist that can be used as a guide in preparing a customized checklist for your institution and operation.

SAFETY TRAINING FOR SUBORDINATES

A safety training program is needed for new and existing employees. The supervisor who is responsible for providing the in-service safety training should

Sidewalks, Steps and Parking Areas

Yes No N.A.

- Are all areas free of conditions which will cause slipping and falling? ☐☐☐
- Is there adequate exterior lighting at night? ☐☐☐
- Are all steps and ramps provided with securely fastened handrails? ☐☐☐

Exits

- Are all exits:
a. free of obstructions and readily accessible? ☐☐☐
b. properly marked with exit signs and lighted? ☐☐☐
c. equipped with an emergency lighting system in good operating condition? ☐☐☐
- Are all exit doors:
a. arranged to open outwards? ☐☐☐
b. easily operated? ☐☐☐
c. provided with anti-panic hardware in all public rooms and exits? ☐☐☐
- Are all fire escapes in good condition? ☐☐☐

Stairs and Doors

- Are all stairs covered with anti-slip surfaces? ☐☐☐
- Are all handrails securely fastened? ☐☐☐
- Are full-length clear glass doors and windows marked to avoid persons walking into them? ☐☐☐
- Are all stairway doors kept closed when not in use? ☐☐☐

Corridors, Meeting Rooms and Public Areas

- Are floor surfaces free of slipping and tripping conditions? ☐☐☐
- Are emergency lighting units in good operating condition? ☐☐☐

Elevators

- Are elevators maintained and serviced on a regular schedule? ☐☐☐
Date of last inspection _____

Deliveries

- Are all delivery trucks inspected and maintained on a regular schedule? ☐☐☐
- Are all drivers experienced and trained in safe driving techniques? ☐☐☐

Housekeeping

- Are adequate ash trays and metal wastebaskets provided in each room? ☐☐☐
- Is combustible trash and rubbish:
a. collected at frequent intervals? ☐☐☐
b. stored in covered metal containers? ☐☐☐
c. disposed of frequently and not accumulated? ☐☐☐
- Are storage rooms neat and orderly? ☐☐☐
- Are flammable paints and liquids:
a. kept to an absolute minimum? ☐☐☐
b. kept in sealed metal containers? ☐☐☐
c. stored in vented metal cabinets? ☐☐☐

FIGURE 9-2. Safety inspection checklist. (Reproduced with permission of the Insurance Company of North America and Pacific Employers Insurance Company.)

Figure 9-2 continued.

	Yes	No	N.A.

■ Are all public areas thoroughly checked for fire hazards after closing? □ □ □
■ Are only non-flammable cleaning fluids used? □ □ □
■ Are all closets free of oil mops and flammable materials? □ □ □

Heat, Light, Power and Appliances
■ Is all heating equipment (including flues and pipes):
a. properly insulated from combustible materials? □ □ □
b. cleaned and serviced at least annually by a competent heating
contractor? □ □ □
Date _____
■ Are electrical, heating and air conditioning rooms:
a. restricted to only authorized personnel? □ □ □
b. free of combustible storage? □ □ □
■ Are there indications of frequent replacement of fuses and/or
resetting of circuit breakers which would indicate overloading of
electrical circuits? □ □ □
■ Are electrical cabinets kept closed? □ □ □
■ Are electrical extension and appliance cords in good condition? □ □ □
■ Has the electrical system been checked and serviced by a competent
electrician within the past year? □ □ □
Date _____
■ Is air conditioning equipment cleaned and serviced annually by a
competent serviceman? □ □ □
Date of last service _____
■ Are all motors kept clean, and adequately ventilated to reduce over-
heating? □ □ □
■ Are all electrical appliances properly grounded? □ □ □

Rest Rooms
■ Are rest rooms cleaned regularly and well maintained? □ □ □

Kitchens
■ Are hoods, ducts, ovens, ranges and filters cleaned on a regular
schedule? □ □ □
■ Is the automatic fire extinguishing system inspected and maintained
by contract? □ □ □
Date _____

Fire Protection
■ Are all fire extinguishers:
a. serviced annually? □ □ □
b. tagged with the date of last service? □ □ □
Date _____
c. conspicuously located and easily accessible? □ □ □
d. hung within 75 feet of any point on each floor except where a lesser
distance is required for a more hazardous area? □ □ □
e. protected against freezing? □ □ □
■ Are periodic tests and inspections made of the following to ensure
their proper operation:
a. fire hoses? □ □ □
Date _____

Figure 9-2 continued.

	Yes	No	N.A.
b. automatic sprinkler system? Date _____	☐	☐	☐
c. fire alarm system? Date _____	☐	☐	☐
■ Is the fire alarm system:			
a. tested periodically? Date _____	☐	☐	☐
b. If manual, marked and accessible?	☐	☐	☐
■ Has fire dept. phone number been conspicuously placed at the switch-board and maintenance shop?	☐	☐	☐
■ Is at least 18″ clearance maintained between sprinklers and high-piled stock in storage?	☐	☐	☐

Employees

	Yes	No	N.A.
■ Are all employees:			
a. instructed to call the fire department immediately in case of fire?	☐	☐	☐
b. instructed in evacuation procedures?	☐	☐	☐
c. instructed in the use of fire extinguishing equipment?	☐	☐	☐
d. instructed on what to do in case of a bomb threat?	☐	☐	☐
■ Are signs displayed on each floor instructing employees and tenants where the emergency exits are located?	☐	☐	☐

Burglary and Theft — Money and Valuables

	Yes	No	N.A.
■ Are all windows, doors, and transoms protected against burglary?	☐	☐	☐
■ Is the cash on hand kept in a burglar-resistive safe which is kept in a well-lighted area visible from the street?	☐	☐	☐
■ Are all outside entrances to the basement kept locked when not in use?	☐	☐	☐
■ Do the delivery trucks have good locks on the merchandise compartments?	☐	☐	☐
■ Is the money on the premises kept near the minimum needed to operate on?	☐	☐	☐
■ Are money collections:			
a. deposited the same day in a bank night depository, or	☐	☐	☐
b. stored in a burglar-resistive safe until deposited?	☐	☐	☐
■ Are valuable items and equipment stored in a safe or vault when not in use?	☐	☐	☐

tailor the program to the audience's needs, based on clearly defined objectives. These objectives should be determined after reviewing the duties and responsibilities of the trainees.

Security personnel job descriptions, although varied, have many common duties and responsibilities. The safety outline, in this chapter, indicates the subjects that should be covered in a safety program for security personnel.

The security supervisor should supplement each session with appropriate hand-out materials and audio-visual aids. An up-to-date listing of films and other safety teaching aids may be secured from the National Safety Council and from other organizations listed at the end of this chapter.

SAFETY TRAINING OUTLINE

Session I

Safety and the Security Officer:

Team Effort; Accidents Affect Morale and Public Relations; Safety—Every one's Responsibility; Accidents are Costly; Company Safety Rules and Regulations; Think Safety.

Session II

General Safety Practices:

Proper Lifting Procedures; Slips and Falls; Ladders; Machine Guards; Skin Protection; Falling Objects; Material Handling; Personal Protection Clothing.

Session III

Identifying Accident Problems:

OSHA Regulations; Electric Hazards; Safety Inspections; Unsafe Conditions; Unsafe Acts; Accident Investigations; Accident Reports.

Session IV

Housekeeping:

Benefits of Good Housekeeping; Security's Responsibility; Sources for Help; Physical Plant—Floors and Aisles; Storage Yards and Grounds; Machines and Equipment.

Session V

Fire Prevention and Control

Identifying Fire Hazards; Causes of Fires; Alarms, Equipment and Evacuation; Fire Drills; Fire Extinguishers; Special Fire Protection Problems.

Session VI

First Aid

First Aid Procedures—Fire Blankets, Stretchers, Telephone Communications; General Medications; First Aid Supplies; Bleeding; Shock; Resuscitation; Breaks and Fractures; Open Wounds; Chemical Burns; Fire Burns; Convulsions.

Session VII

Firearm Safety

Firearm Training; Safe Handling; Loading and Unloading; Maintenance; Control; Horseplay; Storage.

SAFETY TIPS

There are three basic safety attitudes that help prevent accidents. The first basic safety attitude is to always *Think Safety*. The second basic safety attitude is to *Develop Positive Safety Habits*. The third is to always *Act Safely*.

A safe worker accepts the fundamental rules of safety. Ten fundamental rules that develop a positive safety attitude are:

1. Comply with all safety rules, signs, and regulations.
2. Follow instructions. Don't take chances. If you don't know the rule or the proper procedure, ask your immediate supervisor.
3. Correct and/or report all unsafe conditions immediately.
4. Report all accidents. Get first aid promptly.
5. When lifting, bend knees. Get help for heavy loads. (See Figure 9-3 for sample poster.)
6. Don't fool around on any job. Horseplay is a definite <u>NO</u>!
7. Walk, don't run. Excessive haste on stairs and in halls can cause accidents.
8. Have an operational fire safety plan. Conduct frequent fire drills. (See Figure 9-4 for sample poster.)
9. Maintain good housekeeping. Sloppiness can lead to injury and down time.
10. Be knowledgeable of safe work practices and procedures.

ACCIDENT INVESTIGATION

Supervisors have a responsibility to investigate accidents in an effort to control tomorrow's potential losses as well as to help prevent similar accidents in the future. Proper investigation of an accident can lead to the real or basic cause of the accident so that corrective action can be taken to avoid future mishaps (See Figure 9-5).

Not all accidents result in major injuries requiring medical attention. There are those instances commonly known as "near misses" where individuals often escape with minor injuries or no injuries at all. These "near misses" should also be investigated. Today's near miss may be tomorrow's tragedy. Look on accident investigation as accident prevention.

FIGURE 9-3.   How to lift safely. (Reproduced with permission of the National Institute for Occupational Safety and Health.)

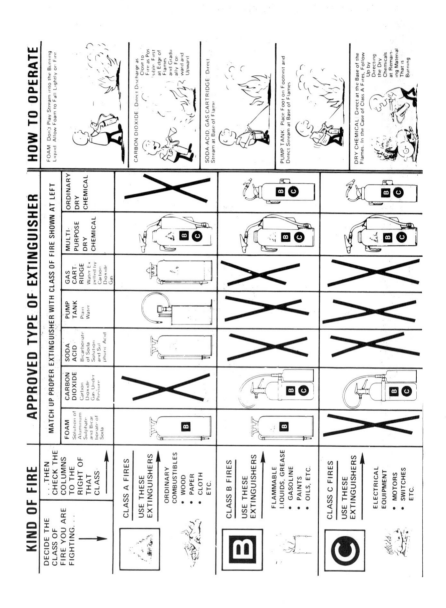

FIGURE 9-4. Poster of an operational fire safety plan. (Reproduced with permission of the National Institute for Occupational Safety and Health.)

MORE EFFECTIVE ACCIDENT CONTROL

THROUGH GOOD

INVESTIGATION   AND   ## REMEDIAL ACTION

BY APPLYING THESE OBJECTIVES

1. To determine all contributing causal factors.
2. To determine the fundamental or basic reason for the existence of each contributing factor.

1. To eliminate or control each contributing cause.
2. To eliminate or control the reason for the existence of each contributing cause.

AND FOLLOWING THESE GUIDEPOSTS

- In case of injury, make sure worker is properly cared for before doing anything else
- When practical, have scene kept as undisturbed as possible
- Investigate as promptly as possible
- Whenever possible, go to scene of accident for initial investigation
- As applicable, have someone else get photographs; make drawings or measurements
- Interview all witnesses, one at a time and separately
- Reassure each witness of investigation's real purpose
- Get witnesses' initial version with minimal interruption; ask for complete version step by step; have them describe and point without doing
- Apply empathy in interviews; make no attempt to fix blame or find fault
- Be objective; don't have fixed opinion in advance
- When witness finishes initial explanation, ask questions to fill in gaps
- Avoid questions that lead witness or imply answers wanted or unwanted
- Summarize your understanding with witness after interview
- Express sincere appreciation to anyone who helped in the investigation
- Record data accurately

(Select appropriate actions)
- Institute formal training program
- Give personal reinstruction
- Institute proper job instruction program
- Institute a safety tipping program
- Temporarily or permanently reassign person/s
- Institute a job analysis program
- Order job analysis on specific job/s
- Revise existing job analysis
- Institute a job observation program
- Order job observation on specific job/s
- Institute new or improve existing inspection program
- Institute pre-use checkout of equipment
- Establish or revise indoctrination for new or transferred employees
- Repair or replace equipment
- Improve biomechanic design of equipment
- Establish biomechanic requirements for new equipment
- Improve basic design or establish design standards
- Improve identification or color code for safety
- Install or improve safeguards
- Eliminate unnecessary material in area
- Institute program of order or improve clean-up
- Institute mandatory protective equipment program or improve existing coverage or design
- Use safer material
- Establish purchasing standard/s or controls
- Institute incident recall program
- Create safety incentive program
- Improve physical examination program

WILL REDUCE

| INJURIES & DAMAGE | DEFECTS & DELAYS |
| REJECTS & REWORK | MISTAKES & WASTE |

. . . . Adequate time spent today on proper investigation and effective remedial action is cost reduction effort on tomorrow's losses.

FIGURE 9-5.   More effective accident control. (Reproduced with permission of the Insurance Company of North America.)

Every accident should be investigated as soon as possible. The sooner an accident is investigated, the better the opportunity to obtain all of the facts. The greater the time span between the accident and the investigation, the greater the chance for information and evidence to be lost, forgotten or destroyed.

Make every effort to investigate the accident at the scene. Make clear to everyone involved that the purpose of the investigation is to obtain the facts and not to place blame. The investigation may uncover human error or negligence, or it may uncover an unsafe condition. The investigation itself, however, should be concerned only with the facts.

The investigation, based on accumulated facts, should determine the cause of the accident. Most accidents have multiple causes or contributing factors. The investigator should endeavor to identify all the causes and contributing factors to determine the overriding cause of the accident. Once the major cause of the accident is determined, make a recommendation to correct the cause of the accident. Submit a report to management indicating the cause and recommended corrective action.

ACCIDENT INVESTIGATION REPORT   .

A written report of an accident investigation should list the facts uncovered during the investigation (See Figure 9-6). It also should include any action taken or recommendations to management. As with all reports, forms differ with each company or organization. A survey of accident reports lists the following essential questions:

- Who was involved in the accident?
- When did it happen?
- Where did it happen?
- What was the cause of the accident?
- What action was taken?

SAFETY CHECKLIST

YES	NO		
☐	☐	1.	I have an operational safety plan.
☐	☐	2.	I am aware of the job safety requirements in my areas of supervision.
☐	☐	3.	I investigate accidents and near misses.
☐	☐	4.	I search, scrutinize and determine methods to control and prevent accidents.
☐	☐	5.	I conduct safety inspections.
☐	☐	6.	I report safety hazards and take preventive action.

SUPERVISOR'S ACCIDENT INVESTIGATION REPORT

COMPANY OR BRANCH	DEPARTMENT
Eastern Packing Company	*Shipping*

EXACT LOCATION	DATE OF OCCURRENCE	TIME	DATE REPORTED
Bldg A. South side, west loading dock	*3-7-69*	*2:45* PM	*3-7-69*

PERSONAL INJURY / PROPERTY DAMAGE

PERSONAL INJURY		PROPERTY DAMAGE	
INJURED'S NAME *Paul S. Riley*		PROPERTY DAMAGED *Lift truck*	
OCCUPATION *Lift truck operator*	INJURED PART OF BODY *right arm*	ESTIMATED COSTS $ *650.*	ACTUAL COSTS $ *785.90*
NATURE OF INJURY *Fracture of upper arm*		NATURE OF DAMAGE *mast and steering column bent*	
OBJECT/EQUIPMENT/SUBSTANCE/INFLICTING INJURY *lift truck*		OBJECT/EQUIPMENT/SUBSTANCE/INFLICTING DAMAGE *ground*	
PERSON WITH MOST CONTROL OF OBJECT/EQUIPMENT/SUBSTANCE *Paul S. Riley*		PERSON WITH MOST CONTROL OF OBJECT/EQUIPMENT/SUBSTANCE *Paul S. Riley*	

DESCRIPTION

DESCRIBE CLEARLY HOW THE ACCIDENT OCCURRED: ATTACH ACCIDENT DIAGRAM FOR ALL MOTOR VEHICLE ACCIDENTS.

Paul was backing lift truck #26 North to clear aisleway in order for truck #22 to pass. He backed into bumping block without applying brakes causing block to break off dock resulting in his truck moving backward off dock to ground 6 ft. below on North side 35 feet from East end. Riley struck arm on truck as he attempted to jump free. He landed clear of truck on ground 6 ft. below dock.

ANALYSIS

WHAT ACTS, FAILURES TO ACT AND/OR CONDITIONS CONTRIBUTED MOST DIRECTLY TO THIS ACCIDENT?

Riley reported defective brake on Operators Report form at start of turn on 3-7-69. He removed truck from garage and operated it from 11 A.M. with defective brake. Operator was using bumping block as stopping mechanism for truck. The bumping block on the dock was in unsafe condition. Condition of block was reported on inspection reports of 1-5-69 and 2-20-69.

WHAT ARE THE BASIC OR FUNDAMENTAL REASONS FOR THE EXISTENCE OF THESE ACTS AND/OR CONDITIONS?

Employee was not properly motivated to recognize seriousness of unsafe brake condition. Garage personnel did not properly follow-up condition on Operators report form. Maintenance control failed to effect prompt corrective action to bumper block. Area supervisor failed to properly follow-up unsafe bumper condition.

LOSS SEVERITY POTENTIAL			PROBABLE RECURRENCE RATE		
☒ Major	☐ Serious	☐ Minor	☒ Frequent	☐ Occasional	☐ Rare

PREVENTION

WHAT ACTION HAS OR WILL BE TAKEN TO PREVENT RECURRENCE? PLACE X BY ITEMS COMPLETED.

X Personnel dept. has been requested to assist in establishing lift truck operators training course. Lift truck rules will be reviewed with all operators by 10-6-69. Riley will be included in both programs when he returns to work. X A statement of policy on handling of safety work orders has been issued by Vice President Matthews. X Maintenance control has issued a hazard classification coding system for use on all safety work orders. X All operators have been properly instructed not to operate equipment considered to be unsafe. X A follow-up system for inspection report items is being developed by Ad Hoc Committee headed by Investigator.

INVESTIGATED BY *Ralph B. Jones*	DATE *3-7-69*	REVIEWED BY *Frank K. Roberts*	DATE *3-8-69*

PH-1231a 100M 10-69 PRINTED IN U.S.A.   INA/PEG ©1969

FIGURE 9-6. Supervisor's accident investigation report. (Reproduced with permission of the Insurance Company of North America.)

YES   NO

☐ ☐   7.   I am acquainted with the safety standards pertaining to personal protective equipment.

☐ ☐   8.   I train my subordinates in accident prevention.

☐ ☐   9.   I inform subordinates of the need for good housekeeping as a safety and fire prevention tool.

☐ ☐   10.   I tell my subordinates how safety rules and regulations are designed to prevent accidents and injuries.

☐ ☐   11.   I demonstrate to my subordinates proper safety procedures.

☐ ☐   12.   I use various training methods to convey safety awareness.

☐ ☐   13.   I encourage my subordinates to ask questions concerning any aspect of safety.

☐ ☐   14.   I evaluate myself to ascertain how fully I meet the requirements of on-the-job safety supervision.

☐ ☐   15.   I make it a practice to give subordinates safety tips.

☐ ☐   16.   I keep up—to—date with safety requirements.

☐ ☐   17.   I make every effort to improve safety conditions within my realm of responsibility.

☐ ☐   18.   I do not tolerate horseplaying on the job.

☐ ☐   19.   I conduct planned fire drills with the local fire department.

☐ ☐   20.   I am knowledgeable in emergency first aid procedures.

SERVICE ORGANIZATIONS AND ASSOCIATIONS

The following list will provide you with an idea of the types of services available. A more complete list of possible sources can be found in the National Safety Council publication titled "Accident Prevention Manual for Industrial Operations."

American Chemical Society
1155 16th Street, N.W.
Washington, D.C. 20036

American Industrial Hygiene Association
210 Haddon Avenue
Westmont, New Jersey 08108

American Medical Association
Department of Occupational Health
535 North Dearborn Street
Chicago, Illinois 60610

American National Standards Institute
1430 Broadway
New York, New York 10018

American National Red Cross
Safety Services
17th and D Streets, N.W.
Washington, D.C. 20006

American Public Health Association
1740 Broadway
New York, New York 10019

American Society for Testing and Materials
1916 Race Street
Philadelphia, Pennsylvania 19103

American Society of Safety Engineers
850 Busse Highway
Park Ridge, Illinois 60068

Human Factors Society
P.O. Box 1369
Santa Monica, California 90406

Industiral Hygiene Foundation of America, Inc.
5231 Centre Avenue
Pittsburgh, Pennsylvania 15232

Industrial Medical Association
55 East Washington Street
Chicago, Illinois 60602

Industrial Safety Equipment Association, Inc.
60 E. 42nd Street
New York, New York 10017

The National Fire Protection Association
60 Batterymarch Street
Boston, Massachusetts 02110

The National Safety Council
452 North Michigan Avenue
Chicago, Illinois 60611

National Society for the Prevention
    of Blindness, Inc.
79 Madison Avenue
New York, New York 10016

Underwriters Laboratories, Inc.
207 East Ohio Street
Chicago, Illinois 60611

PUBLICATIONS AND PERIODICALS

Fire Protection and Control

Fire Engineering. Publisher: Reuben H. Donnelly, 466 Lexington Avenue, New York, New York 10017.

Fire Journal, Fire News, Firemen and Fire Technology. Publisher: National Fire Protection Association, 60 Batterymarch Street, Boston, Massachusetts 02110.

Hazards

Occupational Hazards. Publisher: Industrial Publishing Corporation, 812 Huron Road, Cleveland, Ohio 44115.

Health

A.M.A. Archives of Environmental Health. Publisher: American Medical Association, 535 North Dearborn Street, Chicago, Illinois 60610.

American Industrial Hygiene Association Journal. Publisher: American Industrial Hygiene Association, 210 Haddon Avenue, Westmont, New Jersey 08108.

Chemical Abstracts (Toxicology, Air Pollution and Industrial Hygiene Section). Publisher: American Chemical Society, 1155 Sixteenth Street, N.W., Washington, D.C. 20036.

Industrial Hygiene Digest, Publisher: Industrial Hygiene Foundation, 5341 Centre Avenue, Pittsburgh, Pennsylvania 15232.

Safety

Journal of the American Society of Safety Engineers. Publisher: American Society of Safety Engineers, 850 Basse Highway, Park Ridge, Illinois 60068.

Safety Standards. Publisher: Bureau of Labor Statistics, U.S. Department of Labor, Washington, D.C. 20210.

National Safety News, Industrial Supervisor, Traffic Safety, Journal of Safety Research, Safe Worker, Safe Driver, and Safety Newsletter, Publisher: The National Safety Council, 425 N. Michigan Avenue, Chicago, Illinois 60611.

BIBLIOGRAPHY

Safety Manual for Cooperative Industrial Education, State of New Jersey, Department of Education, Division of Vocational Education, 1976.

Amboroso, Louis J.: "Where Do We Stand With OSHA?" *Security World*, 14(7) 14-59, July, 1977.

Thorsen, J.E., Editor: "Security and the OSHA Act Puzzle," *Security World*, 14(7) 22-25, July, 1977.

Basic Loss Control Kit, Insurance Company of North America.

Key Man Development Program, National Safety Council, 1974.

Supervisor's Safety Manual, National Safety Council, 1973.

Strong, E. Merele, Editor: *Accident Prevention Manual for Training Programs*, American Technical Society, 1975.

Accident Prevention Manual for Industrial Operations, National Safety Council, Seventh Edition, 1974.

Safety Guide for Health Care Institutions, American Hospital Association/National Safety Council, 1972.

10
Community/Public Relations

Effective community relations is measured by public opinion. It is the attitudes and viewpoints others have of the company and the security profession. Community relations is an outgrowth of public relations. It is people—oriented. How we project ourselves, our company and our profession to others determines in great part our respective images. The objective of community and public relations is to foster and maintain a positive public image.

The definition of public relations according to *Webster's Seventh New Collegiate Dictionary*, is "the art or science of developing reciprocal understanding and good will between a person, firm, or institution and the public; also: the degree of understanding and good will achieved."

Using this definition it is obvious that effective public relations requires a degree of understanding and good will. It is something that has to be worked at constantly. As supervisors, it is your responsibility to set the proper public relations example to subordinates.

You must see to it that subordinates:

* Understand the company's, and the security department's, public relations policies
* Accept these policies
* Continuously carry out these policies

IDENTIFYING AND IMPLEMENTING A POSITIVE PUBLIC RELATIONS PROGRAM

The following five steps help in identifying and implementing a positive public relations program:

* Step number one is to identify the public. The "public" is the community at large, employees, visitors to the company premises, and employers.
* Step number two is to assess the public's attitudes toward the security department and the company you serve.
* Step number three is to initiate a positive and continuous public relations campaign. This involves a training awareness program that familiarizes the security staff with the proper procedures for a positive public relations image.

- Step number four requires developing a message to communicate to the "public." Whatever the message, it must be reinforced by positive actions on the job.
- Step number five requires the security staff to diligently work at correcting any negative criticism.

PUBLIC RELATIONS GUIDELINES—STEPS TO FOLLOW[20]

1.   Gather the pertinent information, from inside and outside the organization.

Ask these introspective questions of your organization:

- What are our goals?
- Are we achieving our goals?
- Are our goals realistic?
- How do we see ourselves?
- How would our organization like to be perceived?
- What are our strengths?
- What are our shortcomings?
- What publics do we interact with?
- What publics might be important to our organization in the future?

Get information from outside your organization. From research, surveys, interviews and a frequent review of periodicals and literature evaluate:

- How others see our organization.
- How we relate to our various publics.
- Who is inhibiting achievement of your goals?
- Why?
- What are our points of difference?
- What do we have in common?

2.   Interpret the data.

Define the implications for your group by asking:

- Are changes called for?
- If so, what are they?
- Should we redefine our goals?
- What are we doing that should be done differently?
- What aren't we doing that we should be doing?
- What do we want to happen?
- What is the benefit of having it happen?
- What trends are evident that could affect us in the future?

[20]Reprinted with permission of the Procter and Gamble Co., 1977.

This questioning process calls for:

- Complete objectivity
- The ability to distill from a mountain of information that which is important to you
- Excellent organizational techniques
- Good judgment

3. Recommend appropriate action.

    Determine your objectives:

- Decide what you want to happen.
- Make each objective clear, concise, achievable and measurable.

4. Select the strategy you will use to achieve each goal.

    How do you plan to make each happen? To whom will you make it happen?

    E.g., if one of your objectives is to achieve greater recognition for the security profession in the business community, to have security officers considered for management positions and leadership roles, your strategy might be:

    To reach business thought leaders with success stories on outstanding security officers, to establish recognition of their achievements, management abilities and professionalism.

5. Execute your program.
    Match your media plan to your audience. Communication techniques fall into three categories:

- Publicity—involves the use of mass media (television, magazines, newspapers, radio).
- Face-to-face communications—brings together your own representative, or appointed spokespersons, with members of your target public or with media people who reach those publics. Examples: press conference, convention participation, panel discussion, speaking engagement.
- Good communication method for complicated message or give-and-take format.
- Requires preparation for hostile questions which may distract from your principle message.
- Controlled communications—activities (brochures, booklets, films) in which you have complete control of your message.

    Determine the timing of your program.

- Set up a schedule of items tied to special dates, such as meetings, conventions, etc., which you want to publicize.

- Spread out your efforts over the year, to maintain a continuing flow of communication.

  Appoint personnel.

- Clarify assignments.
- Delegate responsibilities.

  Determine how to measure results, e.g.:

- Pre- and post-attitude surveys.
- Passage or defeat of legislation.
- Extent of media coverage (number of print placements, total air time, audience/circulation count).

6.   Secure feedback.

  Seek measurements on how effective you are; what is working and what isn't; what headway you are making. To do this:

- Keep in direct contact with the thought leaders of your target public.
- Monitor the press, what they are saying about your group.
- Use questionnaires when appropriate—at conventions, meetings, trade shows.

7.   Evaluate the results.
  Compile your results. Measure the results against your goals. Ask your group these questions:

- Did you meet your objectives?
- If not, why not?
- What needs to be changed?
- How should you change it?
- Are your goals still the same?
- Do you have some new challenges?

INTERNAL PUBLIC RELATIONS

You cannot assume that the internal organization, employers and other employees, understand or appreciate what security does in their behalf. It is up to the entire security department to communicate to others within the organization what it does. Telling others about the accomplishments of the security department does not mean bragging or showing off. It does mean honestly informing others about how security contributes to the organization it serves. This is accomplished by communicating information to management and others via report, conferences, speaking engagements, education programs, handbooks, manuals, charts, and posters.

EMPLOYEE ATTITUDES INFLUENCE OTHERS

How security officers view the company for which they work will often influence how their acquaintances, friends and family view the same company. If they speak positively about the company and the security operations, a favorable image will be portrayed to this group. This population, in turn, will probably develop a similar positive attitude and feeling towards the company and the security department.

On the other hand, if security officers speak negatively about the company and the security operation, then those hearing the comments are apt to develop similar negative sentiments. Once a negative sentiment is developed, it is very difficult to change. Countless dollars may be spent to no avail on a massive public relations campaign if those who represent the company and the security department do not support it by word and action. Community relations and public relations, therefore, are everyone's concern.

REASONS FOR POOR RELATIONS

The following are undesirable traits which security officers should avoid. These traits can destroy human relations and adversely affect community/public relations:

- Bad attitude
- Crude speech
- Incompetence
- Griping
- Rumors spreading
- Disinterest
- Irresponsibility
- Impoliteness
- Exploiting people
- Abusive authority
- Failure to communicate

Instruct your subordinates in desirable personality traits, so they understand how their personality traits and their working relations affect themselves and others.

PROFESSIONAL APPEARANCE AFFECTS PUBLIC RELATIONS

Frequently, the security officer is the first person seen when entering a company complex. If the visitor sees a security officer in a sloppy, disheveled uniform, then the visitor's first impression of the company and of the security department will be poor. The visitor's poor impression will be further reinforced and poor public relations developed, if the security officer lacks professionalism, cannot intelligently communicate and respond to questions, or demonstrates bad manners.

Conversely, a security officer will foster a favorable impression if he:

- Is dressed in a clean, pressed uniform or blazer
- Demonstrates a professional attitude
- Intelligently communicates with all parties
- Demonstrates concern and good manners

Furthermore, all security personnel owe it to themselves to be proud of what they do. This pride can be demonstrated in their personal appearance, in their enthusiasm for performing their assignments, and in their sense of accomplishment for a job well done. If a positive attitude prevails within the security force, it will carry over to all those who come in contact with them.

DEALING WITH THE PUBLIC

Most people will respond favorably to anyone who is calm and courteous in their communication process. Even someone who has a complaint, finds it difficult to be abusive to someone who refuses to respond negatively.

A security officer must always be tactful when dealing with others. As a symbol of authority, the security officer must enforce the rules and regulations of the company while being diplomatic in enforcing them. Most people will accept an officer's request for identification in a positive way when the officer is polite. On the other hand, sharp tone of voice or superior attitude will generate resentment. Consider the following. A motorist is about to park his car in a "Fire Zone Area." The security officer is at the scene and informs the motorist that there is no parking in that particular area. The officer could say "Look, stupid, can't you read the no parking sign?" or the officer could say, "Excuse, this is a no parking, fire zone area. There is additional parking in area A or B." In both instances, the motorist will move the car. In the latter instance, the officer's tact allows the motorist to save face and move the car, while the former approach will probably result in some backtalk, wisecrack or obscene gesture from the motorist, and a feeling of hostility that may never be forgotten.

PROJECTING AN IMAGE

Security supervisors are responsible for seeking ways to better inform the public about the security profession. One excellent way to accomplish this objective is to volunteer for public speaking engagements on the subject of the private security field. Schools and service clubs are constantly looking for speakers on many topics. Security supervisors and staff can speak on topics such as:

- A rewarding career in the private security field
- Training requirements for security officers
- White collar crime
- Shoplifting
- Small business security
- Fire security
- Security products and devices

The list of potential topics is endless. The subject matter is interesting. It has broad based public appeal. An interesting presentation by a security officer can, and frequently does, place the security profession in another light. People gain a better insight and understanding of what the field is all about. Their awareness level is increased. The old security guard image can be replaced with a true picture of the field. Informing the public should be a major part of your job. It is also one of the best ways to recruit new members into the field.

COMMUNITY INVOLVEMENT

Community relations requires community involvement. How security personnel interact in the community will determine the effectiveness of their community relations effort.

"Getting involved" is the key to community relations. It means being active in community activities and organizations such as charity drives, emergency rescue operations, coaching in the Little League, and participating on the school board or PTA. It means volunteering your service and talents for the good of the community in which you work or live.

People will get to know you and your occupation as you interact in the community. Comments like "There's Mike, the security officer at XYZ Company, coaching first base," present a positive image for Mike as a person, for the security profession, and for the company. Effective community relations is effective public relations.

TELLING THE STORY

There are multiple facets of public relations—community relations, employee relations, press releases, speaking engagements and special events. The following suggestions, put into practice, will promote effective public relations:

- Write an article for the company newspaper or magazine.
- Make a speech to company officials and/or to company employees..
- Make presentations to outside groups and organizations.
- Prepare a slide-tape presentation on some aspect of the security field or security operations.
- Participate in professional development activities, such as local, state or national conventions or meetings.
- Write an article for the local newspaper on an expansion of services or promotion of an officer.
- Take out "ads" or "boosters" for school yearbooks or civic activities.
- Offer an award or scholarship through your professional association to a deserving recipient.
- Sponsor a sporting activity, e.g., bowling team.
- Prepare brochures on your professional organization. Include facts on the profession's progress and growth.
- Organize a blood donor drive.

COMMUNITY/PUBLIC RELATIONS CHECKLIST

YES NO

1. I project a professional image at all times.
2. I set a positive public relations example for my subordinates.
3. I familiarize my subordinates with the company's and the security department's public relations policies.
4. I diligently work at correcting any negative criticism.
5. I communicate information to management and others on security operations through reports, conferences, etc.
6. I speak favorably to family, friends and acquaintances about the company, and the security department in particular.
7. I avoid undesirable traits that can destroy human relations.
8. I refrain from crudities of speech while on the job.
9. I endeavor to be polite to the public.
10. I maintain the highest standards of personal appearance.
11. I am diplomatic and understanding in my dealings with others.
12. I am always tactful when approaching anyone.
13. I carry out my responsibilities in the highest professional manner.
14. I endeavor to build good will for my company and for my profession.
15. I am determined to achieve greater recognition for the security profession.

YES NO
□ □ 16. I make an effort to accept a speaking engagement at least twice a year.
□ □ 17. I am an active member of a service organization.
□ □ 18. I participate in professional development activities at conventions and meetings.
□ □ 19. I prepare news releases on a variety of security activities that have news interest at the local level.
□ □ 20. I practice the elements of good public relations in all my communication with others.

BIBLIOGRAPHY

Coultier, Richard I.: "Goodby Guard, Hello Joe," *Industrial Security*, October 1971.

Cosentino, Salvatore: *Public Relations and the Hospital Security Officer*, a paper presented at The Fifth Annual Institute for Hospital Security Guards, Greater New York Hospital Association, 1971.

Davis, Keith: *Human Relations at Work*, New York, McGraw, 1962.

Foster, Willard O., Jr.: "The Invisible Alcoholic," *Industrial Security*, 2:9, December 1967.

Goddard, Robert J.: "Professionalism in Security—Fact or Fiction," *Industrial Security*, 9:10, January 1965.

GSA Handbook Physical Protection (PBSP5930.2A) Chapter 9, part 4, "Employment Practices and Requirements," General Service Administration, Washington, D.C., September 1970.

Holcomb, Richard L.: *The Police and the Public*, Springfield, Thomas, 1975.

"How to Tell Your Story," A Communications Handbook on Public Relations, Employee Relations and Advertising, National Consumer Finance Association, Washington, D.C.

Neeson, John V.: "Public Relations and Security," *Security World*, 3(9): 15, October 1966.

Potter, Anthony N., Jr.: "Uniforms and Security," *Industrial Security*, October 1970.

Public Relations Guide, Procter and Gamble Educational Services, Cincinnati, Ohio, 1977.

"Role of the Security Department in Human and Community Relations," *Security Education Briefs* (OAK Security Inc.), Vol. 2, No. 12.

Security Guidelines for Hospitals, The Greater New York Hospital Association, New York, 1968.

"Security Officer—Newly Emerging Specialist in Modern Hospital's Preventive Medicine," *The Cornett* (St. Joseph Hospital, Chicago) 7, No. 8: August 1969. (Appears in Colling, Russell L., Ed.: *Hospital Security and Safety Journal Articles*. New York, Med. Exam, 1970, pp. 26-27.)

Scholl, D.E., Dr.: "Professionalism and . . . You," *Industrial Security*, 9:10, January 1965.

The Police Administration and Public Safety College of Social Science, Michigan State University: *Law and Order Training for Civil Defense Emergency, Student Manual* (Part B), East Lansing, Mich. St. U. Pr, August 1965.

Wathen, Thomas W.: Security Subjects: *An Officer's Guide to Plant Protection*. Springfield, Thomas, 1972.

11

Ethics

Security professionals should adhere to high professional standards of conduct. It is the security supervisor's responsibility to see to it that the personnel under his command are unaware of the Code of Ethics governing security personnel.

The following Code of Ethics should be adopted:

ASIS CODE OF ETHICS[21]

Aware that the quality of professional security activity ultimately depends upon the willingness of practitioners to observe special standards of conduct and to manifest good faith in professional relationships, the American Society for Industrial Security adopts the following Code of Ethics and mandates its conscientious observance as a binding condition of membership in or affiliation with the Society:

I. A member shall perform professional duties in accordance with the law and the highest moral principles.

II. A member shall observe the precepts of truthfulness, honesty and integrity.

III. A member shall be faithful and diligent in discharging professional responsibilities.

IV. A member shall be competent in discharging professional responsibilities.

V. A member shall safeguard confidential information and exercise due care to prevent its improper disclosure.

VI. A member shall not maliciously injure the professional reputation or practice of colleagues, clients or employers.

The Private Security Advisory Council which was initiated by the Law Enforcement Assistance Administration in 1975, developed the following Code of Ethics for the field:

Private Security Code of Ethics[22]

As managers of private security functions and employees, we pledge:

I. To recognize that our principle responsibilities are, in the service of our organizations and clients, to protect life and property as well as to prevent and reduce crime against our business, industry, or other organizations

[21]Reproduced with permission of the American Society for Industrial Security.
[22]Private Security Advisory Council, June 1976.

and institutions; and in the public interest, to uphold the law and to respect the constitutional rights of all persons.

II.   To be guided by a sense of integrity, honor, justice and morality in the conduct of business; in all personnel matters; in relationships with government agencies, clients, and employers; and in responsibilities to the general public.

III.   To strive faithfully to render security services of the highest quality and to work continuously to improve the overall effectiveness of private security.

IV.   To uphold the trust of our employers, our clients, and the public by performing our functions within the law, not ordering or condoning violations of the law, and ensuring that our security personnel conduct their assigned duties lawfully and with proper regard for the rights of others.

V.   To respect the reputation and practice of others in private security, but to expose to the proper authorities any conduct that is unethical or unlawful.

VI.   To apply uniform and equitable standards of employment in recruiting and selecting personnel regardless of race, creed, color, sex, or age, and in providing salaries commensurate with job responsibilities and with training, education, and experience.

VII.   To cooperate with recognized and responsible law enforcement and other criminal justice agencies; to comply with security licensing and registration laws and other statutory requirements that pertain to our business.

VIII.   To respect and protect the confidential and privileged information of employers and clients beyond the terms of our employment, except where their interests are contrary to law or to this Code of Ethics.

IX.   To maintain a professional posture in all business relationships with employers and clients, with others in the private security field, and with members of other professions; and to insist that our personnel adhere to the highest standards of professional conduct.

X.   To encourage the professional advancement of our personnel by assisting them to acquire appropriate security knowledge, education, and training.

In recognition of the significant contribution of private security to crime prevention and reduction, as a private security employee, I pledge:

I.   To accept the responsibilities and fulfill the obligations of my role; protecting life and property; preventing and reducing crimes against my employer's business, or other organizations and institutions to which I am assigned; upholding the law; and respecting and constitutional rights of all persons.

II.   To conduct myself with honesty and integrity and to adhere to the highest moral principles in the performance of my security duties.

III.   To be faithful, diligent, and dependable in discharging my duties, and to uphold at all times policies and procedures that protect the rights of others.

IV.   To observe the precepts of truth, accuracy and prudence, without allowing personal feelings, prejudices, animosities or friendships to influence my judgements.

V.   To report to my superiors, without hesitation, any violation of the law or my employer's or clients regulations.

VI.   To respect and protect the confidential and privileged information of my employer or client beyond the term of my employment, except where their interests are contrary to law or to this Code of Ethics.

VI.   To cooperate with all recognized and responsible law enforcement and government agencies in matters within their jurisdiction.

VIII. To accept no compensation, commission, gratuity, or other advantage without the knowledge and consent of my employer.

IX.   To conduct myself professionally at all times, and to perform my duties in a manner that reflects credit upon myself, my employer, and private security.

X.   To strive continually to improve my performance by seeking training and educational opportunities that will better prepare me for my private security duties.

The essential elements in a Code of Ethics are outlined below:

E   (enforcement of rules and regulations; equality; efficiency; exemplary conduct)

T   (tolerant; trustworthy; thorough)

H   (helpful; honest; human understanding)

I   (ideals; incorruptible; insight; impartial)

C   (confidentiality; Code of Ethics; character; crime prevention; compassionate; courteous)

S   (self-restraint; self-control; skill development; standards)

SET A POSITIVE EXAMPLE

Security officers look to their supervisors for direction. The supervisor sets the example. If a supervisor does not adhere to high ethical standards, his subordinates might loosely adhere to ethical standards. On the other hand, a supervisor with high ethical standards sets a positive image for his subordinates to emulate.

Supervisors should demonstrate, and encourage their men to follow these characteristics:

Honesty.   This should be the backbone of a security officer's character. The security officer should be absolutely honest in all things. The security profession is based on the honesty of its officers.

Fairness.   A security officer should demonstrate fair treatment to all people. Personal feelings and prejudices should never influence a security officer's decision. He should be impartial in his decision making process.

Courageous.   A security officer should be counted on to carry out his professional duties even under trying conditions. In the face of danger he should be courageously calm.

Self-discipline.   A security officer should maintain control of his temper at all times. He should discipline himself to correct any bad habits which would impede his progress.

Loyalty.   A security officer should diligently discharge the duties entrusted to him. He should take personal interest in the welfare of his company and the people he serves.

Trustworthy.   A security officer must be trusted to maintain the confidentiality of his employer. Information entrusted to him must remain confidential.

GRATUITIES

Gratuities are defined as something given in return for service. Security officers should never accept gratuities. Most firms, and nearly all local, state, and federal government agencies absolutely forbid any employee to receive gratuities of any kind.

Security officers should never place themselves in a compromising position by accepting even a small gift. Officers who accept favors such as meals, coffee, and gifts are often known as "moochers." While it may not be illegal, it is compromising. "Mooching" breeds contempt, even from the individual providing the handout.

Officers who accept small favors and gifts can develop a "you owe me" attitude. It's the first step in rationalizing that they deserve something extra for their services. This kind of attitude can lead to accepting bigger and bigger gifts until they seriously compromise their self-respect, integrity, and position as a security officer.

CONFLICT OF INTEREST

Security supervisors are responsible for enforcing the company policy in conflict

ETHICS

of interest situations, such as dual employment, kickbacks, leaking company secrets, gratuities, etc. The policy regarding what constitutes a conflict of interest situation should be clearly spelled out in the employee manual. This information must be disseminated to all employees so that they are aware of the acceptable practices within the terms of their employment.

THE SECURITY OFFICER'S PRIVATE LIFE

Security officers are expected to adhere to an acceptable moral code, on and off the job. The security officer's character has to be such that people will recognize that he behaves as an honest man all the time. He cannot be honest on the job and dishonest in his personal life. Double standards, especially in so vital an area, cannot be tolerated in the security professional.

Because of the nature of the job, people accept a security officer in one of two ways:

1. As an individual for what he is
2. As a security officer and the image that he represents

If the private life of a security officer is out of line with his professional life, people may lose confidence in his professional judgment.

The values spelled out in the Code of Ethics must be demonstrated in the security officer's personal life as well as in his professional life. In many respects, the security officer is expected to demonstrate more regard for acceptable moral values than would be expected from the average citizen. If a security officer is an alcoholic, people wouldn't say "there goes Joe the drunk." They will say "there goes Joe the drunken security officer." This casts a negative image on the entire security profession.

Security officers should be careful not to engage in excessive gambling, drinking or sexual promiscuity. Any one of these excessive behaviors off the job can compromise the security officer on the job. Security officers can be blackmailed into performing illegal deeds on the job through any of those behaviors. The security officer is also expected to pay his debts, treat all people with respect, obey all laws, respect family life, and respect the rights of others regardless of race, creed, color or national origin.

ETHICS CHECKLIST

YES NO
☐ ☐ 1. I treat all people fairly, showing no partiality for friends, relatives, and acquaintances.

YES NO

□ □ 2. I demonstrate exemplary conduct becoming an officer both on the job and in my personal life.

□ □ 3. I accept no gratuities regardless of the source offering them.

□ □ 4. I am impartial in my decision making process.

□ □ 5. I am honest in all my professional undertakings.

□ □ 6. I can be trusted with information that must remain confidential.

□ □ 7. I remain courageously calm in the face of danger.

□ □ 8. I obey all the regulations of my organization and I obey all the laws governing society.

□ □ 9. I demonstrate a positive rather than a negative behavior.

□ □ 10. I pride myself in being self-disciplined.

□ □ 11. My actions and deeds are honorable in nature.

□ □ 12. I am diligent in discharging the duties entrusted to me.

□ □ 13. I adhere to the precepts of truth, accuracy, and prudence.

□ □ 14. I promote programs that will raise the standards and efficiency of the security field as a whole.

□ □ 15. I do not use my position to solicit gifts or favors.

□ □ 16. I do not permit personal feelings, prejudices, animosities or friendships to influence my decisions.

□ □ 17. I am fair to all parties regardless of their social position, race, or creed.

□ □ 18. I maintain a compassionate respect for the dignity of all individuals.

□ □ 19. I strive to maintain self-control even when pushed to the limits.

□ □ 20. I never subject anyone to any form of cruel, inhuman or degrading treatment.

□ □ 21. I strive for perfection in all of my undertakings.

BIBLIOGRAPHY

A Guide to Security Investigations, American Society for Industrial Security, Washington, D.C., 1970, pp. 36-37.

Hill, Ivan: "Honesty, Freedom and Business Ethics," *Security Management,* Vol. 23, No. 9, September 1979, pp. 53-60.

Kooken, D.L., *Ethics in Police Service.* Springfield, Illinois, C.C. Thomas, 1959.

Munro, Jim L.: *Administrative Behavior and Police Organization,* Cincinnati, W.H. Anderson, 1974.

Niederhoffer, Arthur and Abraham S. Blumbers, ed.: *The Ambivalent Force: Perspectives on the Police,* Waltham, Massachusetts, Ginn and Company, 1970.

Olivet, George and Doyle, Edward: *Transactional Analysis.* Police Department City of New York.

Training Key #42, *The Police Image,* I.A.C.P. Inc., Washington, D.C., 1969.

Watson, Nelson A.: *Issues in Relations.* Gaithersburg, Maryland, I.A.C.P., 1973.

Appendix

Certified Protection
Professional Program*

PURPOSES

The program of certification of security professionals has the following objectives:

- To raise the professional standing of the field and improve the practice of security management by giving special recognition to those security practitioners who, by meeting prescribed standards of performance, knowledge and conduct, have demonstrated a high level of competent and ethical practice.
- To identify sources of professional knowledge of the principles and practices of security and loss prevention, related disciplines, and of laws and regulations governing or affecting the practice of security.
- To encourage security professionals to carry out a continuing program of professional development.

ADMINISTRATION

The ASIS certification program is administered by the Professional Certification Board (PCB), which consists of nine members appointed by the President of ASIS for terms of three years each. The PCB has full and final authority to judge the qualifications of each candidate for certification.

A Certification Program Administrator is responsible for the operation of the certification program.

An Examination Administrator will administer each examination. The responsibilities of this position will be carried out by individuals selected by the PCB.

*The Certified Protection Professional Program is reproduced with permission, American Society for Industrial Security, Washington, D.C.

The PCB has no intention of determining who shall engage in security management. That a person is not certified does not indicate that he or she is unqualified to perform security responsibilities, only that such person has not fulfilled the requirements or has not applied for certification. *Membership in the American Society for Industrial Security is not required for certification.*

ELIGIBILITY PREREQUISITES

Each applicant must meet the following basic standards:

Experience and Education:

A.   Ten (10) years of security experience, at least half of which shall have been in responsible charge* of a security function** or

B.   An earned Associate's Degree from an accredited college and eight (8) years of security experience, at least half of which shall have been in responsible charge of a security function, or

C.   An earned Bachelor's Degree from an accredited college or university and five (5) years of security experience, at least half of which shall have been in responsible charge of a security function, or

D.   An earned Master's Degree from an accredited college or university and four (4) years of experience, at least half of which shall have been in responsible charge of a security function, or

E.   An earned Doctoral Degree from an accredited college or university and three (3) years of security experience, at least half of which shall have been in responsible charge of a security function.

*"Responsible Charge" shall mean that charge exercised by an individual who makes decisions for the successful completion of objectives without reliance upon directions from a superior as to specific methods or techniques. An applicant need not have held a supervisory position, as long as the position(s) on which the application relies shall have included responsibility for independent decisions or actions.

**"Security Function" shall mean the protection of assets.

Examples of acceptable experience in a security function are:

1.   Experience as a security practitioner in the protection of assets, in the public or private sector, criminal justice system, government intelligence or investigative agencies, *at least half of which* shall have been in responsible charge of a *security function.*

2.   Experience with companies, associations, government, or other organizations furnishing services or equipment, including consulting firms, shall be considered as meeting the experience requirements; provided the duties and responsibilities substantively relate to the design, evaluation and application of systems, programs or equipment, or development and operation of services for protection of assets in the private or public sectors. Direct sales experience alone will not be considered as qualifying experience.

3.   Experience as a full-time educator on the faculty of an accredited educational institute shall be considered as meeting the experience requirements, provided the responsibilities for courses and other duties relate primarily to knowledge areas pertinent to the management and operation of protection of assets programs in the private or public sectors.

ENDORSEMENT

Each application for certification as a Certified Protection Professional shall be endorsed by a member of the Professional Certification Board, or a person who has already been certified as a Protection Professional. Endorsement of an application for certification shall signify that the person making the endorsement is satisfied that the statements by the applicant on the application for certification are complete and accurate; and that in the judgment of the person making the endorsement, the applicant is eligible for certification.

PLEDGE TO MAINTAIN STANDARDS OF CONDUCT

The applicant must affirm adherence to the following Code of Professional Responsibility. These standards are based on the ASIS Code of Ethics.

- *I will* endeavor to perform my professional duties in accordance with the highest moral principles.
- *I will* work vigilantly and unceasingly to thwart the activities of individuals or groups who seek to change or destroy the democratic government processes by force or violence or by any other unlawful means.
- *I will* strive to strengthen my government by the security of facilities and conserving of resources.
- *I will* be faithful and diligent in discharging the duties entrusted to me, protecting the property and interest of employers and safeguarding the lives and well-being of employees.
- *I will* observe strictly the precepts of truth, accuracy, and prudence.
- *I will* respect and protect confidential and privileged information.
- *I will* promote programs designed to raise standards, improve efficiency and increase the effectiveness of security.

SUCCESSFUL COMPLETION OF EXAMINATIONS

Written examinations will be required for all applicants who meet the experience/ education and responsible charge criteria. Successful achievement of passing grades on a battery of tests, shall be necessary. This battery covering twenty-one subject areas, shall include: eight (8) mandatory and four (4) chosen by the applicant from the optional subjects on the theory and principles in the following fields of security protection and loss prevention:

Mandatory Subjects

1. Emergency Planning
2. Investigations

3. Legal Aspects
4. Personnel Security
5. Physical Security
6. Protection of Sensitive Information
7. Security Management
8. Substance Abuse

Optional Subjects

1. Banking and Financial Institutions
2. Computer Security
3. Credit Card Security
4. Department of Defense Security Requirements
5. Educational Institutions Security
6. Fire Resources Management
7. Health Care Institutions Security
8. Manufacturing Security
9. Nuclear Security
10. Public Utility Security
11. Restaurant and Lodging Security
12. Retail Security
13. Transportation and Cargo Security

PROCEDURES

Application forms may be obtained from the Program Administrator at the ASIS Headquarters, 2000 K Street, N.W., Washington, DC 20006, and filed with the appropriate fee at any time.

The applications will be reviewed and, if it is in order, the applicant will be sent information on the examinations, included a selected bibliography listing appropriate material for study.

Written tests will be administered at appropriate times.

The results of the examination will be scored by an official of the PCB or its designated agency representative.

A candidate who has failed the written examination, must wait one calendar year before taking the examination again.

All details pertaining to requests and results concerning certification will be handled on a confidential basis, except the awarding of certification to successful candidates will be publicized.

Upon successful completion of all requirements, an applicant will be certified and a certificate with the applicant's name and individual number will be forwarded to that person.

Certification will be in effect for three years and, unless the certified individual applies for and meets requirements for recertification, will expire on the day following the third anniversary of the original certification.

RE-CERTIFICATION

The principal purpose of the CPP program is professional improvement. Continuing education and participation in professional endeavors are necessary for all who are involved with professional security management. A re-certification program has been designed to encourage individuals to keep current in new security developments and active in security programs. Therefore, to remain certified, a Certified Protection Professional must be re-certified each three years with the accumulation of six (6) professional credits during the three year period.

MAINTENANCE CREDIT

		Credits
A.	Membership (non profit professional association)	
	1. Membership in ASIS	1 per year
	2. Membership in other chartered security organization (Supporting data required)	1 per year
B.	Educational Programs and Courses	
	1. Attendance at each ASIS Annual Seminar	1 per year
	2. Attendance at another security conference or convention of two days or more (Supporting data required)	1 per year
	3. Attendance at an ASIS Headquarters sponsored Workshop	2 per year
	4. Attendance at an ASIS Security Institute course (except Certification Review course)	3 per year
	5. Successful completion of a security course at an accredited college or university (Supporting data required)	2 per credit hour
	6. Attendance at ASIS recognized courses presented by government or private organizations (For each 40-clock hour course)—(Supporting data required)	3 per year
C.	Service as an Officer, Board Member, Regional Vice President, Committee Chairman or Committee Member in a chartered security organization or association.	
	1. Each year served as an officer of ASIS	3 per year
	2. Each year served as a member of ASIS Board of Directors, as a Regional Vice President or Committee Chairman	2 per year

3.	Each year served as an ASIS Committee member	1 per year
4.	Each year as an ASIS Chapter officer	2 per year
5.	Each year served as an ASIS Chapter Committee Chairman	1 per year
6.	Each year served as an officer of a chartered security organization or association (Supporting data required)	3 per year
7.	Each year served as a Board member or Committee Chairman of a chartered security organization (Supporting data required)	2 per year

D. Speeches, Instruction, and Other Program Participation

1.	Each appearance as an instructor, seminar or workshop leader at an ASIS educational program or at another security seminar (Supporting data required)	1 per seminar
2.	Each presentation as a panelist in an ASIS or other security organization program (Supporting data required)	1 per seminar
3.	Regular instruction in a security topic at an accredited college or university (Supporting data required)	2 per credit hour taught
4.	Guest instructor on a security topic at a college or university or other recognized educational institution (Supporting data required)	1
5.	Guest speaker on a security topic at an ASIS Chapter Meeting (Supporting data required)	1
6.	Guest speaker on a security topic at a civic organization meeting (Supporting data required)	1

E. Published Articles and Other Literary Contributions

1.	Each security article published in *Security Management* or other national publication (Supporting data required)	1
2.	Each security book review published (Supporting data required)	1
3.	Published articles, monographs, booklets and contributions to books on security subjects (Supporting data required)	1 to 3 (Open based on judgement of PCB)

F. Others

Points will be considered on any special accomplishments the certified applicant requests, e.g., invention, legislative appearance, special recognitions, etc.

REVOCATION OF CERTIFICATION

A.   Certificates are subject to revocation by the PCB for any of the following causes:
  1.   The individual certified shall not have been eligible to receive such certificate, irrespective of whether or not the facts were known to, or could have been ascertained by, the PCB at the time of issuance of such certificate; or
  2.   The individual certified shall have made any misstatement of fact in the application for such certificate or any other statement or representation, connected with the application for certification; or
  3.   The individual so certified has been found to have engaged in unethical practices or has been convicted of a felony.

B.   No certificate shall be revoked unless the following procedures are followed:
  1.   A copy of the charges against the CPP and the information concerning the event or events from which such charges have arisen is sent by registered mail to the individual.
  2.   The CPP is given at least 20 days to prepare a defense.
  3.   A hearing is held on such charges, before an official designated by the PCB, at which time the person is given a full opportunity to be heard in his or her own defense including the right to cross-examine witnesses appearing and to examine documents material to said charges.
  4.   A majority of the PCB in official session called on due notice shall find the individual not eligible for continued certification and direct the PCB Administrator to issue such notice signed by the Board's President.

Index